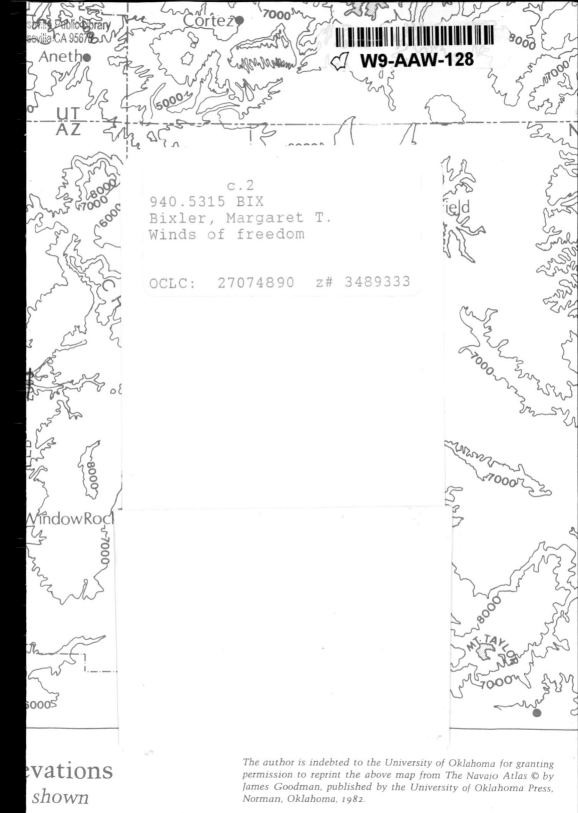

WindowRoc

vations

shown

The author is indebted to the University of Oklahoma for granting permission to reprint the above map from The Navajo Atlas © by James Goodman, published by the University of Oklahoma Press, Norman, Oklahoma, 1982.

Oklahoma Press

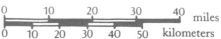

Winds

of

Freedom

The Story of the Navajo Code Talkers

of World War II

by Margaret T. Bixler

TWO BYTES PUBLISHING, LTD.

2002

Copyright 1991 by Margaret T. Bixler
First Printing June 1992
Second Printing March 1995
Third Printing June 2002

Original Cover Art by Helen Sickels Allen
Cover Graphics and Layout by Peter Manchester

Produced by
TWO BYTES PUBLISHING, LTD
P.O. BOX 633
STRATFORD, CT 06615-0633

ISBN:1–881907–00–7 (hard cover edition)
1–881907–01-5 (soft cover edition)

*Printed and Published in
the United States of America*

Dedication

Table of Contents

APPENDICES

List of Illustrations

Preface

No one knows for sure where the quest for food, shelter and protection began for the early Navajos. No trails remain. There are signs, however, that the history and culture of today's Navajo Indian tribe go back uncounted centuries. The round head, flat face and nose, straight black hair and the narrow shape of the eyes resemble the Chinese, especially those from the Mongolian area.

Archaeologists are also struck by the similarities of early Indian artifacts to the designs and carbons of Mongolian and Tibetan artifacts. Lacking other evidence we can speculate that Navajo Indians began evolving in what is now China. How, then, did the Navajos find their way to their present Holy Land in the southwestern United States? Again, no one knows for sure. Perhaps for reasons of drought, famine, warring tribes or a combination of all three, the Navajos found their way across a land mass (now the Bering Strait), migrating from Siberia or Outer Mongolia, through areas of Alaska and Canada.

There is evidence in the Navajo language that The People, or *Diné*, as the Navajos call themselves, mingled with the northern Eskimo, particularly the Athabascan-speaking tribes. Not surprisingly, the Navajo and Athabascan languages can be understood by both tribes. Linguistic evidence seems to indicate that the Navajos broke from their Athabascan ancestors in Canada about 1000 a.d. and started drifting southward. The reason may have been an ice-free corridor into the area they now occupy. This corridor, perhaps, continued to grow warmer with the recession of the Ice Age, and the Navajos may have wanted an area for better hunting and farming. Because their language was not fully written down until the mid-twentieth century, the history, arts and culture of the Navajos were handed down by word of mouth, by words written by foreigners in a foreign tongue, by song and dance, and by a way of life very

Beautiful Monument Valley on the Navajo Reservation is situated in north-ern Arizona. Although much of the surrounding land has eroded through the years, these majestic monoliths remain in stark testimony to their ancient beginnings.

different from that of peoples in Anglo-Western cultures.

The unraveling of Navajo prehistory remains the task of archaeologists and other scientists. As the cocoon unfolds to reveal its butterfly, so will an understanding of the Navajo heritage reveal to us the character and propensities of the Code Talkers. We see the winds of change come both to the Navajos and the Anglos. The first two chapters of this book go briefly into the colorful history and fascinating prehistory myths as told to Navajo children.

This way one can appreciate the sacrifices of a remarkable group of men known as the Code Talkers of World War II. Theirs was the only code the enemy could not break. Their contribution to the war in the Pacific theater was summed up by one Marine colonel in this way:

> "The United States would not have won the Battle of
> Iwo Jima had it not been for the Code Talkers."

These brave youths, many underage and coming from a "foreign" culture into the Anglo war culture of the Marine Corps, were able to adapt, to integrate, and yet to retain their beliefs in the *Navajo Way.*

Changes were inevitable, and World War II is often considered a "coming out" of the Navajo Nation. The Holy Winds were blowing. Freedom of the Navajo people to believe as they wished and freedom for their land to remain holy would be the ultimate goal.

Perhaps a 1992 update on the use of the name "Indian" interchangeably with the term "Native American" would be in order: In this writing, both terms are used. When I visited the Reservation in 1991, Columbus Day was being celebrated throughout most of the United States, although not on the Reservation.

In one office a posted sign was pointed out to me:

"Indians discovered Columbus."

The word, "Indian," did not seem to be a derogatory term by any of those persons I visited; however, I do see some apparent confusion with the citizens of India. Perhaps "Native Americans," the term used in Civil Rights legislation, will become the popular term of the future.

Helen Sickels Allen

Rock art, in the form of petroglyphs and pictographs, abounds in the Southwest. There are those who do not consider such art to be writing or message sending, rather that it is a communication with the supernatural to ensure prosperity, good hunting, good health or plenteous rain for crops.

On the other hand, the belief prevails that the art, especially in the form of groups of figures, does tell a story and records important events that took place before the advent of a written language as we know it.

Perhaps both ideas are relevant to those early times and should be taken into account by today's history scholars.

One can never fully understand another's culture, for culture is never static. It constantly changes with the passing of time, the implementation of new-found skills and the intermingling of other cultures. Beliefs change. Even the *Navajo Way* has evolved somewhat from its ancient beginnings. As an Anglo, I am an outsider attempting to look in at a complicated, sophisticated, unwritten and totally different culture–that of the Navajos. At times, therefore, I may appear to undervalue, to misunderstand, or to misread

According to some of my Navajo friends, I have undervalued the *Navajo Way* and its influence on the Navajos and the Code Talkers. It is true the the archaeological view of how and where the Navajos arrived in the present world does not take into account the more spiritual viewpoint. I have tried in Chapter II to present, although very briefly and – sad-to-say – inadequately, the worlds and the ways through which the Navajos traveled and learned. These stories and myths must be taken into account as we evaluate the culture from which the Code Talkers came. Today many Navajos believe in the spiritual approach and look to the words contained in the dedication of this book:

> *Your cultural heritage–*
> *Your spiritual orientation–*
> *Your willingness to forgive–*
> *Your love of family–*
> *Your belief in the Web of Life–*
> *The "Navajo Way" gives hope to a world in need.*

History, however, can be visited from many viewpoints. Writing from one perspective need not negate a different perspective. Only when we encircle historical events, can we really arrive at the truth. It is in this light that I present my view of the Navajo Code Talkers. My hope is to convey to the reader something of the background, the war experiences and the changes that came about as a result of the sacrifices of a group of young Navajo men uniquely involved in World War II.

From the Author's Photo Album

These are the author's informal pictures of teachers and students at the Presbyterian Church's Nursery School on the Reservation, Ganado, Arizona.

Standing left to right: Dr. P. J. Van Dyke, Joe Perry, Rose Perry, Barbara Van Dyke, Alberta Lane.

Introduction

IN JANUARY 1980, part of my graduate studies in Humanities at the University of New Haven (Connecticut), was planning a field study on the Navajo Reservation in Arizona. Having read several books before leaving Connecticut and perusing several more on the plane to Arizona, I assumed my main purpose on the Reservation would be to get to know The People, or *Diné*, as the Navajos refer to themselves. Certainly this was, and still is, the most exhilarating part of my visits. As I grew to know and like the people I met, I also began to realize that here was a culture vastly different from my own in its history, language and understanding of nature and life. I wanted to know more–and not from books alone. I wanted to hear from the people themselves something of what they believed and how they lived their daily lives. Because Navajos are usually silent, taciturn and immune to the advances of an aggressive stranger, my information was found through friendly informal talks. Sometimes it was necessary to sit in companionable silence listening to one's own thoughts and ideas. There were many who took time from their own lives to sit and talk with me and to answer what must have seemed like naive questions.

My special thanks go to two Navajos, Howard Gorman and his wife, Grace, who introduced me to the *Navajo Way*. Howard's explanations of a Navajo pre-history of which I had little knowledge will be discussed in Chapter II. As we sat on the floor, Grace demonstrated the art of weaving with a small loom upon which she made tabletop-size rugs. One particular rug designed with a different pattern on each side was beautiful, unusual and time-consuming to make. Such work is seldom for sale, but, as Grace indicated, she would keep this rug for her own pleasure or give it as a gift.

Thanks, too, go to Brenda Colter, a teacher in the public school in Ganado. One day I became a teacher's helper in her sixth grade classroom. Brenda asked me to bring along anything of Connecticut that I had. Pictures of Connecticut and of my family helped open the conversation. Soon I found myself being interviewed. Two of her slower students were assigned to me for remedial reading in English. It was here I began to understand how long it takes for the Navajo-speaking child to learn to comprehend English. Brenda's class gave me the realistic insights I needed to pursue my own readings on the subject. After school, Brenda told me some of her frustrations in teaching a sixth grade class, most of who were at the fourth grade level. Despite the difficulties, her obvious pride in these students showed as she shared their writings about a nature field trip they had taken. On this topic her Navajo students were superlative!

Dr. Irvy Goossen, a well-known and highly respected Anglo teacher of the Navajo language, took time from the house he was building to introduce me to the intricacies of the Navajo language. His information was not only technical, but it also enhanced my understanding of the cultural differences between the Navajos and the Anglos.

Joe Perry helped me understand the Star Gazer and the Trembling Hand diagnosticians that, in turn, gave me a better understanding of the medicine man. His wife, Rose, and their friend, Alberta Lane, described every-day life on the Reservation.

Dr. Gerald Yost, now working at The Phoenix Medical Center, and his wife, Carolyn, became my friends. Dr. Yost was instrumental in clarifying the relationship of the doctor to the medicine man.

Carolyn Brown spoke of life on the Reservation. For her, it is different as she is a single parent bringing up three children, one of them handicapped. The tribe is in the process of building a home for her. The first site selected was abandoned because a *kiva*, or place of assembly, was found while digging the foundation. While a new site is being located, she continues to cope with inadequate living quarters. Through it all, Carolyn is a particularly warm and courageous Navajo.

The Daltons, Karl and Etta, opened their unconventional and up-to-date *hogan* and let me look around. As Mr. Dalton told me the story about how his home was built, I learned about the Navajo feeling of responsibility towards one another. Mr. Dalton, an older man, was building his *hogan* by himself. Unknown to him, he was being observed by a young Indian. One day the young Indian appeared and said: "You will kill yourself" and, according to Mr. Dalton, the young man finished the *hogan* almost by himself. The young Indian's picture occupies a place of honor in the *hogan* and in the heart of Karl Dalton.

Dabah Dobrinen, a Navajo who was raised off the Reservation by adoptive Anglo parents, shared with me her Master's thesis on the Navajo Community College. She also shared some insights into her own frustrations in bringing up her two sons on the Reservation in a culture to which she was not accustomed.

Margaret Nicholin graciously spoke about the work of the Ganado Alcoholic Program (GAP) and showed me the facilities. The patients lived at the facility and participated in Occupational Therapy in two small factories. One group made simple pine coffins and the other specialized in silk screening. Medical problems were handled at a nearby hospital. Time was also given for informal talking and meeting with counselors. Unfortunately, probably for economic reasons, the facility was closed in 1989.

Another debt of gratitude goes to Dee Hershberger, a teacher of English as a second language. When she heard of my interest in the Code Talkers, she introduced me to Mary Stuart Sparle, a columnist for the *Arizona Republic*. Mary is also a public relations expert who produced a television program about the Code Talkers. She took it upon herself to arrange contacts for me and shared all her notes, pictures and mementos.

Through Mary I met James Dawkins, a Marine in World War II. Jim has been made an honorary member of the Navajo Code Talkers' Association. Through stories of his continuing friendship with many of the Code Talkers, I learned of some of the great accomplishments of the Code Talkers as Marines in the war and after. His insights brought new understanding into some of the cultural adjustments the Code Talkers faced in a new and different world after the war.

Benis Frank and Dan Crawford of the Reference Department in the Marine Corps Museum, Washington, DC, sent me the final version of the Code as used by the Code Talkers, known as *The Navajo Code*, when it became declassified. This dictionary is found in its entirety in Appendix C.

Dr. Stuart Struever, founder and director of the Crow Canyon Archaeological Center in Cortez, Colorado has been invaluable in the later revisions of this work. He set up seminars both on and off the Reservation from which I, as a participant, learned substantially more about the Indians (Native Americans), their strengths and their problems. He further recommended readings and even shared unpublished scientific writings with me.

Matthew Hall, a lawyer and trusted friend, read and critiqued my "first" manuscript. He gave me insights very necessary to telling the story of a unique group of men.

I wish to give extra thanks to those who have been most closely involved:

First, to my supervising professor, *Dr. Ralf E. Carriuolo*. His sincere interest in my field study encouraged and inspired me to delve deeper.

Second, and Third, to *Dr. P. James Van Dyke and his wife, Barbara (my sister)* who from 1980–1985 lived on the Reservation. It was in their home where I ate most meals and slept, and found the informal conversations with the Navajos. Through Jim and Barbara countless interviews were set up; and through their many efforts this book is now written and published.

And, especially, *to my family: my daughter, Katharine Holt*, patient and helpful with many readings and who did an excellent job of proofreading; *my son, David*, who chauffeured and supported me on my 1991 rounds on the Reservation, in addition to critiquing the manuscript; and most particularly, to *my husband, Roland*, who has through this entire project been enthusiastic, steadfast and lovingly encouraging!

There were so many others who gave of their time and energy to assist me in this project; among them:

Albert Smith, the 1992 President of the Code Talkers' Association, for his willingness to call special meetings of the Association, to critique some of the early page proofs of this manuscript;

Code Talker Dr. Carl N. Gorman and his wife, Mary E. Gorman, who although taking exception to some of what is written herein, nevertheless took time to counsel me on many pertinent points;

the Day Nursery School teachers at the Presbyterian Church in Ganado;

Mary Graham, head librarian of the Heard Museum in Phoenix;

Marty Post, head librarian of the Cook Christian Training School in Tempe;

Della Dye of the Marriott Library Special Collections Division at the University of Utah;

the doctors and nurses at Sage Memorial Hospital on the Reservation; and,

Richard Hill, who not only read and critiqued the manuscript but also put me in touch with my editor and publisher, Elizabeth Clark.

The author is also indebted to the University of Utah for granting permission to use quotations for Chapters III–VI of this book from the Doris Duke Oral History Tapes, hereafter referred to as Doris Duke Collection, Manuscript Nos. 953, 1111, 1121, 1122, 1143, 1145, 1146, 1147, 1156a, 1158, 1159, 1160, 1161, 1162, 1164, 1165, 1166, 1168, 1171, 1223, 1457, 1458, Manuscripts Division, Special Collections, University of Utah Marriott Library, Salt Lake City, Utah 84112.

MARGARET T. BIXLER

*Winds
of
Freedom*

Now a Navajo Tribal Park, these Monument Valley monoliths rising from the valley testify to the awesome beauty of the Reservation.

Another scenic wonder of the Navajo Reservation is Canyon de Chelly, pronounced "de Sha." Within this "rock canyon" (detailed photo–top of page 5), the Anasazi carved their homes. Later, the Navajos lived and sought sanctuary here. Parts of the Canyon are still used for living and farming.

CHAPTER 1

The Beginnings

"First there was the beautiful and rugged land.
And then came the people to the land
and they called themselves *Diné*"
from *The Book of the Navajo*[1]
by Raymond Friday Locke

THE LAND IS stark and beautiful. It is high plateau country with canyons, arroyos, and mesas where the San Juan River meanders westward to the Colorado. Pinons, junipers, spruce and majestic ponderosa grow in abundance above 4,000 feet. Snow-capped peaks over 11,000 feet tower above the plateau adding to nature's splendor. Beneath the high plateau there is low desert. The climate is dry. And water is scarce. The surrounding mountains soar above the desert floor. This is the great Southwest of the United States that includes present-day Arizona, New Mexico, and parts of Colorado, Utah and California.

It is here the story begins about a group of Navajos who became known as the Code Talkers. Despite the deep roots in their culture and ancestral lands, they left the beauty and isolation of their home on the Reservation to help the United States in World War II. Through the Navajo language they developed the only code the enemy was never able to decipher. The very isolation and uniqueness of their culture, and, in turn, a language that was passed along orally from generation to generation, became the crucial means by which they gave their military assistance. So, it becomes necessary to gain an understanding of their culture in order to understand their sacrifices and contributions.

This region is where archaeologists have found three major cultures of the prehistoric period: the Anasazi, the Mogollon and the Hohokam.[2]

The Anasazi, the *ancient ones*, inhabited the northern plateau highlands, that area that is now northern Arizona from Flagstaff north to southern Utah, and from Albuquerque in New Mexico north into southwestern Colorado. Around the time of Christ, these early basket makers developed a rudimentary form of dry farming. In addition to farming, the Anasazi were builders. Chaco Canyon is resplendent with the awe-inspiring ruins of this ancient civilization. Roads were built with timbers, carried by hand, from as far away as 30 miles. The ruins of huge stone apartment houses still dominate the area, echoing with them the mysteries of the centuries.

Other Anasazi groups wandered the northern plateaus of the Southwest seeking the best areas for growing corn. Life with its many hardships was not easy for these people. There were seasons when the crop failed and the domesticated turkeys and dogs, both used for food, died. Many of the people were plagued with disease. Ancient skeletons have been found which show the presence of arthritis. These adversities, however, brought about a technical progress that was reflected in the highly developed Anasazi villages.

This is one of the two tiered Anasazi ruins found in Canyon de Chelly. The rock "path" from one tier to the other is treacherous, but easily walked by young sure-footed Navajos.

The ruins, in the photograph above, shows the detail of "apartments", built by the Anasazi, are similar to those found in Canyon de Chelly.

Sarbo

These ruins in Canyon de Chelly, known as the White House ruins, are signs of early dwellers abandoned around 1300 A.D.

A cornfield on the Navajo Reservation. Corn is one of the renewable re-sources that the Navajos look to for food. Much of the land of the cornfields has been taken over for mining, a non-renewable resource. While the mining provides jobs and money for the tribe, there is a point of view that questions this use of the land for future generations.

There are indications that there was trade with the natives of what is now Mexico. Macaw feathers from this area, or possibly from the Hohokam culture, have been found in Utah. Copper bells and iron pyrite cubes set in bitumen to make mirrors are typically Mexican. Trade with the people of California and other areas also seems likely. Abalone shells in decorative form have been found among Anasazi ruins.

Nevertheless, despite the evidence of their cultural advancements, the Anasazi abandoned their villages and all but disappeared around 1300 A.D. The reason for their departure is usually attributed to drought, severe climate/natural disasters, and use of natural resources or possibly an invasion by a hostile group. After their disappearance there were few other peoples present, although the Pueblos continued to live to the South. Wandering Navajo and Apache tribes were able to inhabit such former Anasazi places as Canyon de Chelly. There, many centuries later, one of the prominent Navajo Code Talkers would be born and brought up.

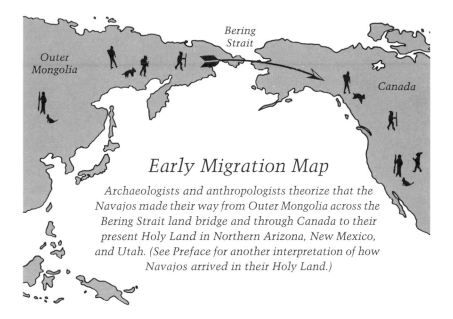

Early Migration Map

Archaeologists and anthropologists theorize that the
Navajos made their way from Outer Mongolia across the
Bering Strait land bridge and through Canada to their
present Holy Land in Northern Arizona, New Mexico,
and Utah. (See Preface for another interpretation of how
Navajos arrived in their Holy Land.)

Even though many anthropologists consider the present-day
Hopi as Anasazi descendants, it seems likely that the Navajo may
have known the Anasazi before the so-called disappearance, if we
are to believe stories handed down from the elders to their children. The Towering House Clan of the Navajos takes its name
from living with the Anasazi people of Kin Yaa'a Towering House
region. Other clans[3] may have intermingled and joined the Towering House as well. When the Navajo says the Anasazi are his
ancestors, he may in part be correct. In addition, it is noteworthy
that the interpretation of the word "Anasazi" is the *ancient ones*
or, literally, *those who have gone before.*

Barney Mitchell, writing in *Between Sacred Mountains*[4] says
that his grandfather, a well-known medicine man, didn't understand why the Anasazi were considered foreign to the Navajos. He
felt that the Navajos, as they moved from area to area, intermingled with the Anasazi. In time the Anasazi learned to speak the
Navajo language and called themselves "Navajos." And so, as
Mitchell says, "You can't point back in time and say, 'Here the
Anasazi ended and there the Navajos began.'"

To the South of the Anasazi homeland, and in the eastern and northeastern mountains of present-day Arizona, was a group of people known as the Mogollons. The Mogollons and the Anasazi are thought to be the ancestors of the present-day Pueblos. Pueblo influence is strong among the Navajos. At one point after the Spaniards arrived it was necessary for the Pueblos and the Navajos to live and work together for their own protection.

The Mogollons were the first to establish houses and to develop pottery. Vessels have been found that didn't leak and burn up when water was boiled. These utensils date back to 200 B.C. The Mogollons were the first to use the bow and arrow, and may have passed it on either by accident or by design.

The third great prehistoric group of the Southwest is the Hohokam. The Hohokams were canal builders. Many of the irrigation canals in and around Phoenix are extensions of ancient Hohokam canals.

The disappearance of the Anasazi, the Mogollons and the Hohokam left a vacuum in the area that was quickly filled by the arrival of various nomadic hunters from the North. These nomads were the Navajos and Apaches who had probably come down an ice-free corridor from the Athabascan territory in the northern parts of present-day Alberta, Saskatchewan and northwestern Manitoba in Canada.

While there are no written histories (the written Navajo language

Isaac Wood Dugan

Navajos refined and perfected the art of silversmithing learned from Mexicans. Their jewelry and ornaments are known and admired throughout the world.

is a product of the 20th century), scientific evidence seems to indicate that centuries before these nomad tribes had come from the area of Mongolian China. There may even be evidence that their roots go even further south into India, according to historian and teacher, Dr. Kusum Patel. As they searched for food, shelter from the cold and protection from warring tribes, they eventually found their way across the land bridge (now the Bering Strait) into present-day Alaska. As the Navajo and Apache tribes continued their search for a homeland, they absorbed characteristics and especially the language of the Athabascan tribes living in the area they passed through (what is now present-day Canada). Prehistory myths of the Navajos tell us there were at least four worlds through which The People (*Diné*) had to travel before reaching their present Holy Land.

Into this background the Europeans arrived in 1540. Francisco Vasquez de Coronado, by virtue of having married into royalty, was appointed governor of one of the provinces of New Spain (now

During the many wars and wanderings of the Navajos, hiding places were needed. These ruins are on the edge of a deep gulch. Opposite the gulch and on the top of a mountain are more substantial ruins which today can be reached only by rope ladder.

Mexico). News about cities of great wealth to the North prompted Coronado to arrange an expedition. Instead of the seven cities of gold, he found nomadic groups of people he called "Querecho": In all probability these people were the Pueblos, the Navajos and most probably the Plains Apaches.

The accounts of Coronado are of great historical value. He relates, for instance, the discovery of a new kind of oxen, wild and fierce. No doubt these were the buffalo, which at one time roamed as far west as the Rio Grande, hunted and revered by the nomadic tribes of the area. The buffalo became a valuable resource with many uses: its meat for food, its skin for building teepees, making clothes and moccasins, its sinew for bows and tools for sewing, its dung for fuel, its bones for awls and its bladder for water containers. Nothing was wasted, an indication of the Indians' extreme

Grandmothers still sit in hogans or outdoors (when weather permits) after dying and spinning wool to finally weave the beautiful rugs so highly prized by collectors.

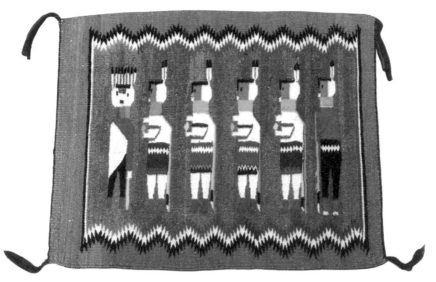

The unusual rug, pictured above, depicts Yé'ii Bicheii dancers. More commonly, rugs have geometric designs made up by the weaver herself.

reverence for life and the Circle of Life as they found it. Although the buffalo has long since disappeared from the West, it is still celebrated in song and dance by the Navajo, Hopi, and other Pueblos.

The arrival of the Spaniards did change life in the Southwest. They found no horses, no sheep, no fruit trees, no marks of civilization as they knew it. Knowledge, ideas, tools, and religion were exchanged between the Indians and the Spaniards. Silver was mined in the Mexican area before the Spaniards came. But they were the first to bring the precious metal to the Indians. However, smithing in iron, brass and copper preceded smithing in silver.[5] Its beauty, worked by the Navajo silversmith, is still worn proudly today by Indians and Anglos alike.

The Navajo and Apache Indians, both Athabascan-speaking, began to evolve in different ways. Fray Alonso de Benevides, a Spanish priest, pointed out that the Navajos were hunters and gatherers, and the Apaches were farmers, particularly dry farming. It is probable that, as a result of the close relationship with the Pueblos, the Navajos developed a sedentary farming type of existence that is typical of the Pueblos. In contrast, however, the Western Apaches became the more war-like Indians noted for their fierce fighting abilities. Trafzer,[6] in his book, *The Kit Carson Campaign*, says that the name "Apache" comes from the Tewan word *"apache"* meaning enemy or stranger and the name *Navajo* comes from the Tewa word *"nabaju"* meaning people of the great planted fields, further illustrating the growing difference between the two groups. Although earlier Anglos preferred to spell the name of the tribe in the English mode *"Navaho,"* today the tribe uses the Spanish *"Navajo."* This is the official name in the treaties with the United States. Today the tribe prefers the name, *"Diné"*.

In addition to farming, the Navajo began the raising of livestock–horses, cattle and sheep; but in order to acquire horses and sheep, Navajo raiding parties attacked the Spaniards and the Pueblos. Code Talker R. O. Hawthorne tells of his grandfather who would go from Wide Ruins to Roswell. There he would kill the Mexican sheepherders, take the sheep and horses and bring them back. According to his grandmother, that is how the present-day herds of the Navajos began. While it may be true that this marauding was only done by a certain few, it could not be tolerated by the United States Army and did eventually lead to the battle with Kit Carson and to the surrender of the entire Navajo Nation in 1864. This was followed by the Long Walk (over 300 miles) to their incarceration at Bosque Redondo (Fort Sumner or *Hwééldi*), New Mexico.

During the 1600s the Navajos became known for their fearsome raids. At that time they probably could have driven the Spaniards from the area had they wanted to. In addition to the Spaniards and the Pueblos, the Hopis and the Zunis (the largest Pueblo tribe) were considered enemies of the Navajos. In 1680 the Pueblos finally carried out a successful revolt against the Spaniards. After this revolt some of the Navajos and the Pueblos began to cooperate for protection.

From 1700 until 1850 the Navajos experienced periods of war, then peace, then war again. It was also a time of expansion. The Navajos adapted quickly to new ideas. They became innovators, building on new ideas and making them their own. The weaving arts of the Pueblos, for instance, were adopted by the Navajos, as

Canyon de Chelly is one of the most beautiful natural wonders of the South-west. The land at the bottom of the Canyon was good for farming and a gentle stream provided water. The Canyon also was a good hiding place, and Carson had no idea how many Navajos were hidden within its walls.

as they designed their own distinctive rugs for which they are justifiably famous today. The horse, brought by the Spaniards but developed more fully by the Navajos, allowed the invading Navajo culture to survive. The Pueblos, because they were a sedentary tribe, did not use the horse to its fullest potential.

In the area of language, the Navajos were more rigid. They seldom learned the language of another tribe, preferring to keep their Navajo language intact. Indeed, other tribes and some Anglos learned Navajo in order to communicate. It is this language upon which the Navajos based their code, used in World War II, and which so baffled and confused the enemy.

When the White Man (Anglo) invaded the Southwest Territory, the Navajos were only loosely organized with many headmen. The common enemy forced them to join together as a united Navajo Nation. This union caused consternation among United States officials when the territory was annexed after the Mexican War of 1848. The obsessive expansion of the United States into the Southwest made the idea of a nation within a nation offensive to the Anglo.

Now the Navajo became subject to the laws and Constitution of the United States. While the Spaniards had hoped to integrate the Indians into their culture, the Anglos saw the Indians as a barrier to the progress of expansion.

General James H. Carleton assumed command of the New Mexico territory in 1862. He was a Christian who thought he was a humanitarian. He believed firmly in the reservation system to confine the Indians and determined to put it into effect.[7]

General Carleton needed help with his campaign to resettle the Navajos and the Apaches on reservations. He enlisted the aid of Kit Carson, a young man who had run away from home in Missouri and joined a wagon train headed for Santa Fe. Craving excitement, Carson had joined the Army to fight the Confederates. He was easily impressed by a man like Carleton who had the social graces that Carson lacked. Thus began the Kit Carson campaign against the Navajos, the Navajo surrender and the Long Walk to Fort Sumner. Carleton and Carson had underestimated the resistance of the Navajos. In December 1863 Carleton decided to send Carson to do a final round-up of the Navajos and invade their stronghold. This final invasion took place at Canyon de Chelly.

In order to defeat the Navajos, Carson sent scouting parties into the Canyon and effectively destroyed the crops. The Navajos, with their bows and arrows, were fighting the guns of Carson's men. During the winter of 1863–64 the Navajos were starving. Their only recourse in 1864 was to surrender and walk the 300 or more miles to Bosque Redondo (Fort Sumner), 180 miles south of Santa Fe, New Mexico, to be relocated or to attempt to escape. Many were killed, some did escape, but several thousand began the Long Walk.[8]

The stories of the hardships and tragedies of this period in the Navajo history have been told and retold to Navajo children. Now the Navajo Community College in Tsaille, Arizona has published the stories of forty Navajo men and women whose parents and grandparents survived the Long Walk.[9]

Howard Gorman, whom I interviewed in Ganado in 1980, gave the Navajo view of the Carson raids as one in which the soldiers arrived unexpectedly to destroy the water wells, burn the cornfields and the peach orchards. "We were not warlike," says Gorman, "but, still, we had these soldier visitors."

Gorman's published story describes the hardships of the walk:

> On the journey the Navajos went through all kinds of hardships, like tiredness and having injuries. And when those things happened, the people would hear gunshots in the rear. But they couldn't do anything about it. They just felt sorry for the ones being shot. Sometimes they would plead with the soldiers to let them go back and do something, but they were refused. This is how the story was told by my ancestors. It was said that those ancestors were on the Long Walk with their daughter, who was pregnant and about to give birth. Somewhere beyond K'aalogii Dzil (Butterfly Mountain) on this side of Bilin (Belen), as it is called, south of Albuquerque, the daughter got tired and weak and couldn't keep up with others or go any further because of her condition. So my ancestors asked the Army to hold up for a while and to let the woman give birth. But the soldiers wouldn't do it. They forced my people to move on, saying that they were getting behind the others. The soldiers told the parents that they had to leave their daughter behind. "Your daughter is not going to survive, anyway; sooner or later she is going to die," they said in their own language. "Go ahead," the daughter said to her parents, "things might come out all right with me." But the poor thing was mistaken, my grandparents used to say. Not long after they had moved on, they heard a gunshot from where they had been a short time ago. "Maybe we should go back and do something, or at least cover the body with dirt," one of them said. By that time one of the soldiers came riding up from the direction of the sound. He must have shot her to death. That's the way the story goes.

In the view of many Navajos who recorded their ancestors' reminiscences of the Long Walk, the Navajos themselves were to blame for their problems. They had sent warring parties to kill the Utes who were considered enemies; they raided the Pueblos and the Mexicans and brought back their sheep and horses. These actions, some Navajos feel, may have brought on the war with the United States Army as well as with the other Indian tribes.

Living in confinement at Fort Sumner was difficult for the Navajos. Hunting was permitted but there were very few horses. Sheep were also scarce. Firewood, also in limited supply, could only be found at great distances and soon was exhausted. At this time in history the Navajos found themselves alone. The Spaniards were gone (although the Mexicans still raided) and the United States Army had sworn to put down the Navajo warring parties. But as one reads the stories of the Long Walk period, one is struck by the close relationship of The People to their Holy People (deities). Even at Fort Sumner ceremonies were held. The Holy Ones were believed to be responsible for the decision of the United States to permit The People to return to their own land. Despite the many hardships, the Navajo retained their basic culture and their integrity.

Finally, in April 1868, after four years of confinement at Fort Sumner, several Navajo leaders were allowed to go to Washington and confer with President Andrew Johnson. On June 1, 1868, the Navajo leaders signed the "Treaty Between the United States of America and the Navajo Tribe of Indians" (Naaltsoos Sani or Old Paper). At long last the Navajos were allowed to reverse their Long Walk and return to their beloved Holy Land. Many lives had been lost but the Navajo Wars had come to an end.

The first part of this important treaty of 1868 dealt with the law: United States law would be obeyed and certain crimes would be handled by the Federal Courts. After signing this treaty, the United States would consider the Navajos as a Navajo Nation. They would be allowed to make their own laws and to enforce them for the Navajos living on Navajo land, as long as such laws had the approval of the United States Government.

The major part of the treaty dealt with the land area. Herein lies a basic problem. The Navajo does not understand the concept of land ownership. He does not "own" land, rather he uses land as he needs it. The Europeans, on the other hand, are landowners. The idea of using only the amount of land one needs for grazing, farming or hunting, without regard to fences or boundaries, is incomprehensible to the Anglo. Therefore, the idea of the Reservation with its boundaries was not understood by the Navajo. It was necessary for them to accept the idea of the Reservation in order for them to remain on their holy territory.

The history of the United States Government with regard to the Navajo Reservation has not been completely honorable. Certain sections of the land have been added, then taken away when desired by mining companies or by use for railroads, then when mining companies found nothing or railroads chose alternate routes, the land was given back. Some Navajo land was sectioned off and given to ranchers as homesteads. Still other land was given to the Hopis for their Reservation. The Hopi claim they were using this land before the Navajo. Because the land is holy to both tribes, many problems have ensued. Unfortunately, the treaty did not mention water rights. Often land on which springs were found was owned by others, thereby making grazing land of little use without water.

The treaty also said the Navajos should continue farming, and therefore they would receive seeds and farm tools. Free English education for Navajo children was promised. The Navajo leaders began to realize that treaties and laws would now be written rather than agreed to verbally; thus, the Navajos found it necessary to send their children to school.

Today there is very little left of Fort Sumner on the Pecos River. It has been acquired by the State of New Mexico as part of the Museum of New Mexico. Should it be abandoned and forgotten, or should that remaining be preserved as a monument to man's inhumanity and oppression? The Navajos have not forgotten They had accepted the Anglo treaty, they had not accepted Anglo ways. They had kept their culture, their beliefs, their ceremonies and their way of living.

The prehistory myths and legends are still told to Navajo children and are kept as a unique part of Navajo life. Even though seventy-five years would elapse before the Japanese would attack Pearl Harbor, this very culture–the *Navajo Way*–would shape the Navajo soldier as he once again went off to war to defend his Holy Land.[9]

Notes on Chapter I

1. Locke, Raymond Friday, *The Book of the Navajo* (Mankind: Los Angeles, 1976), p. 7.
2. Linda S. Cordell, *Prehistory of the Southwest* (Orlando, Florida and London: Academic Press, Inc., 1984). Linda Cordell also lists a fourth, the Patayan. Cordell points to the sites in the Colorado River Valley as typical of this fourth culture. As yet there is little known of this group but archaeologists suggest that this tradition is "ancestral to the modern Yuman-speaking tribes."
   In 1891, J. W. Powell classified the Indian Linguistic Families of America North of Mexico. Powell found 58 specific families with many subdivisions. Although this has been reduced by combining and some modifications, Powell's classifications have remained. The present-day Yuman-speaking family consists of the Yavapai, the Havasupai, the Walapei, and the Mohave tribes. An edited edition of this listing is published by the University of Nebraska Press (1966). We shall also be concerned with another great linguistic family: the Athabascan. The Navajos and the Apache tribes are members of this family and can understand each other if the speech is slow and enunciated clearly.
3. For further information on clans, see Chapter II.

18

4. Mitchell, Barney, *Between Sacred Mountains* (Tucson: Sun Tracks and University of Arizona Press, 1984), p. 83.

5. Adair John, *Navajo and Pueblo Silversmiths*, (Norman University of Oklahoma Press, Norman, OK, 1944).

6. Trafzer, Clifford E., *The Kit Carson Campaign* (Norman: University of Oklahoma Press, 1982).

7. Trafzer, Clifford E., *The Kit Carson Campaign* (Norman: University of Oklahoma Press, 1982), p. 231.

In General Carleton's words: "To gather them together little by little onto a Reservation away from the haunts and hills and hiding places of their country, and there be kind to them: there teach their children how to read and write: teach them the art of peace; teach the truths of Christianity. Soon they will acquire new habits, new ideas, new modes of life: the old Indians will die off and carry with them all latent longings for murdering and robbing; the young ones will take their places without these longings: and thus, little by little, they will become a happy and contented people, and Navajo Wars will be remembered only as something that belongs entirely to the Past."

8. *Navajo Stories of the Long Walk Period* (Tsaille, Navajo Nation, Arizona: Navajo Community College Press, 1973).

9. In 1998 after carefully reading the second printing of this book, Mary Gorman (wife of Carl Gorman, philosopher and statesman of the Navajo Nation and former Code Talker) takes exception to some of the "historical" statements in Chapter I. She feels strongly that the religious approach or the *Navajo Way* is the only correct approach to Navajo history. Her comments are much appreciated and aid in giving the reader a broader view for a deeper study of the Navajo culture. I have made some changes at her suggestion. However, Winds of Freedom is not meant to be a history book but only a brief study to give some understanding of the complicated culture out of which the Code Talkers came.

10. For further reading I recommend most enthusiastically Henry and Georgia Greenberg's book, *Power of a Navajo, Carl Gorman: The Man and His Life* (1996: Clear Light Publishers, 823 Don Diego, Santa Fe, New Mexico 87501).

Hogans Come in Various Shapes

CHAPTER II

The World of the Code Talkers

PRIOR TO WORLD WAR II, life on the Reservation remained simple, still dominated by long-standing Navajo customs. Radio and television had not yet brought the outside world to the Reservation. Most young men had the typical Navajo hairstyle that had never been cut. Many of the main roads were not yet paved. The tracks that passed for back roads were used mostly for horses or horse and wagon. The forked stick or "male" *hogan*, now rarely seen, was originally used as a dwelling and for Blessing Way ceremonies. The "female" rounded *hogan* replaced the forked stick male *hogan* for all ceremonies and became the dominant dwelling.[1] The Navajo creation–the emergence–and the fascinating stories of how the Navajos should live–the *Navajo Way*–were handed down through many generations from grandparents and parents to their children. The legacy of the Long Walk was ever present.

There was only one Navajo doctor on the Reservation. The few Reservation hospitals were ill-equipped and staffed mostly by Anglos. The medicine man, on whom most Navajos relied, was considered a "witch doctor" by many outsiders and not welcome in the hospital. As we shall note later, at least one of the Code Talkers was largely responsible for the change in attitude among both doctors and medicine men that would take place later.

The Reservation was a private world, a world of beauty, of great silences, of contemplation. In that beauty and silence one's whole world and the way of looking at the world could be changed. I doubt that there is a Navajo child or adult who does not know, and believe, the chant given below:

> *All is beautiful before me*
> *behind me*
> *below me*
> *above me*
> *all is beautiful all around me.*

This covers all,
the mountains
whose ways are beautiful,
  the skies
    the waters
      the darkness
    the dawn
whose ways are beautiful,
  whose ways are beautiful
    all around me.[1]

This identity with the land is important. Life is as ruggedly beautiful as the land. Humans are a part of the land–and a part of nature. The Navajo conclusion that man does not have dominion over nature is a fundamental difference between the Navajo and the Anglo. The Anglo assumes that his desire to have superiority over other humans and animals is part of "human nature."

At the start of World War II, Navajo families lived in isolated "camps." Many still do. These camps, usually at a distance from the highway, are not villages or communities as the Anglo knows them. They are living and farming headquarters for the extended family that is made up of father, mother, children, grandparents, and any other relative who wants to live there.

In each camp, there is a *hogan*: a one-room house made of logs and mud often with a mud floor, a center pit for fire and an opening in the top for smoke. The *hogan* comes in many shapes, sometimes round, more often with five or more sides. There are no windows and one door that always faces East. In prehistoric times Talking God (the god of the East to whom the Navajo prays in the early morning) showed the people how to make a *hogan*. Since all prayers start in the East with Talking God, it is important that the door always face this way. In addition to the *hogan*, each camp usually has other dwellings: a more conventional house, perhaps a house trailer and often a summer home made of forked boughs so that air can circulate freely. The original *hogan* may then be used as a ceremonial or "male" *hogan*. As other members of the extended family come to live, other *hogans* and/or dwellings may be added to the camp.

On several occasions I have been invited to a ceremonial *hogan* for dinner. Before partaking of the feast, we had to cleanse our inner bodies with a drink of water. Then, in Navajo, we prayed for the cleansing of our souls and a safe return to our homes.

My conversation with Shonto Begay[2] illustrates better than I can the preferred isolation of these camps. During the week, Shonto lives in Kayenta so that his children can attend school and his wife can pursue her career in child development. On the weekend, he retreats to his grandmother's modified *hogan* and his own new "camp" in the high plateaus. Shonto is well educated, holding a Master's degree, and makes a living by selling his paintings.

Far across the valley from Shonto's weekend home is the coal mining area of Black Mesa with its huge coal chute that can be seen for many miles. In this land of beauty and mysticism one might presume that the commercial aspect of the coal mine–its tearing apart of the land–would bother Shonto. To the contrary, he

Sarbo

Navajo shepherd tends his flock.

23

knows the coal is needed and therefore is mined. Instead, it is the lights on the coal chute, kept burning 24 hours a day, that he can see across the valley at night that disturbs him. They shatter the peace and tranquillity of his world, as he looks out at the beauty of the nocturnal universe.

Just as the buffalo was revered in prehistoric times, the sheep has taken on great meaning to the Navajo. Shepherds and shepherdesses view their sheep as friends in every sense of the word and know each one of them by name. Over the years, the sheep corral has become a necessary part of the Navajo camp because sheep are useful for so many things. Their wool provides yarn for weaving rugs and blankets. When butchered, the sheep provide food and their sheepskins provide warmth in winter. It would be an insult to the Navajo's friend, the sheep, if any part of the animal was discarded.

Alberta Lane,[3] a shepherdess, told me the story of one of her friends. His flock was stolen so he searched everywhere, finally finding it about to be auctioned. When he tried to claim the flock, the auctioneer challenged him with, "How do you know these sheep belong to you?" "Because I know their names," was the answer and, to prove it, he called out the name of one. The sheep responded and came to him. The sad ending of this story is that he had to buy the sheep from the auctioneer because he had no further proof that they were his. Alberta knew her sheep by name, too, and when we parted she was leaving to bring her sheep back to the corral for the night. Alberta and I did not say good-bye in the Anglo custom nor did we say "au revoir" in the French sense. Navajos do not gather for small talk, but rather for specific purposes, such as the business of trading or engaging a medicine man. Leave-taking, therefore, means that the business is accomplished and the word, if any, is *"Hágoónee"* (So Be It).

In this matrilineal society when a Navajo girl marries, her husband comes to live with her family. Any inheritance is through the woman. In prehistoric times, according to Navajo myth, it was Changing Woman (derived from the changing seasons) who spawned all the tribes. She was raised by First Man and First

Woman but was not their child. No one knows who her mother was. From Changing Woman comes the tradition of the man going to live with the woman's family. The concept of family (and the extended family) has remained the number one priority for Navajos throughout the generations.

Navajo myths affect not only the relationship of the mother to the family but also the relationship of the father to the family. Twins, fathered by the Sun, were born to Changing Woman. The first Twin was born as lightning struck in the East, West, North and South. He was the stronger of the Twins and named Slayer-of-Alien-Gods. He was meant to kill the monsters which at that time inhabited the earth. The second Twin was born to the sound of gentle thunder. He was named Child-of-the-Water, the peaceful one.

The Twins wished to meet their father, the Sun, but on their journey they met with many obstacles. However, they were helped by Talking God who gave them a rainbow sprinkled with white, black, blue, pink and yellow medicine. Gifts of black, white, blue and yellow stone flint were used to support the webs of Spider Woman so that she was not able to entrap the Twins during their journey. The Wind helped the Twins obtain bows and arrows. Prayersticks made of reed, given by the Fire God, were placed where the gods could see them. When the Twins finally arrived at the Sun's house, they were repulsed several times by the Gate-keepers. Until proving themselves worthy, they could not be accepted by their father. After surmounting the many obstacles placed in their way, the Sun finally recognized the Twins as his own. Now the Sun became very helpful. He gave them gifts and assisted them in performing their assigned tasks of slaying the monsters and making the earth safe.

This is typical of the relationship between father and child in the Navajo culture. Gary Witherspoon[4] explained this relationship as one of both distance and assistance. As the sun is distant from the earth, yet protective and necessary for proper growth, so the Navajo father is both distant and protective of his children. The mother, on the other hand, is close to her children as is Changing Woman to the earth.

More than one son of a Code Talker mentioned this combination of closeness and separateness with his father. He remembers certain times of closeness–short-lived but ideal–when they cooked meals together on the Reservation. The rest of the time there was little communication as the father separated himself from his family (part of that separation was his World War II service in the Marine Corps). Today father and son are very close. They have taught each other much, and the father is very proud of his son.

Another aspect of this unique mythical culture is the Navajo attitude toward death. As a part of the Navajos' belief in the Web of Life, it would seem that death is accepted as a part of nature. While this is essentially true, death releases the evil spirits and, therefore, it is to be feared. Many Navajos will have nothing to do with the dead or dying. I heard the story of a Navajo boy who always hid in a nearby burial ground when he was bad. He knew his parents, because of the myth, would never come to get him. When someone died in a *hogan*, the building was abandoned and usually burned. Elderly people traditionally went into the desert to die if they knew their time was approaching.

Land ownership on the Reservation is somewhat complicated and has created some problems with county and state lines. The Reservation land belongs to the Navajo tribe, but the federal government in Washington holds the land "in trust" for the Navajos. This means the Secretary of the Interior is in charge of the land and administration is in the hands of the Bureau of Indian Affairs. Except for some "private" lands, which generally are not part of the Reservation, land ownership is not held by the individual.[5] Land, as well as all of nature, is to be used for the benefit of everyone and everything. One does not "own" land, one uses it. Land belongs to the family only for farming and grazing. It cannot be given away or inherited, except that the extended family may continue to use it as long as it is needed. The wife can pass the land's use to her daughters and their husbands. Sheep and other animals are owned in a somewhat similar manner. Animals are assigned to a certain family member. Up to a point, it is not considered moral for a person to sell the animals in order to buy something special for oneself, such as a pick-up truck that is a prized possession on the Reservation.

The Anglo concept of time is not easily understood in the Navajo mind. According to Dr. Irvy Goossen,[6] the Navajo divides his day into parts. At daybreak, it may be necessary to do certain chores or to say certain prayers. The rest of the day is divided according to what needs to be done. The Navajo eats when he is hungry, sleeps when he is tired. He does not feel the regimentation of three meals at certain times, or hours of work, or certain hours for sleeping that the Anglo feels.

According to Carl Gorman, the Navajo concept of time is a space/time continuum whereas the Anglo deals with a linear sense of time. There is no original word for "number," except *volta* that means "that which is counted." If the Navajo-speaking people learn numbers at all, they will usually learn English numbers. Goossen gives this example of the cumbersome way Navajos would literally translate "1967": *One thousand and added on to it nine one hundreds and added on to it sixty and added on to it seven.* There simply is no short way to read "1967." The appearance of numbers throughout Navajo chants and sandpaintings expresses profound concepts.

Of the Navajo families I have met, most of the members now help to maintain the family unit. However, traditionally, they are neither expected nor forced to work. Tending sheep was often done by one of the older women or the young son or daughter. Weaving was usually done by an elderly grandmother who, in turn, would be the teacher for her daughter or granddaughter.

Navajos are bound to each other in a clan system in connection with the extended family. There are sixty-four clans and each Navajo is related to many of them. The relationship is always through the mother whose clan becomes the main clan. The Navajo is born into this clan. He is born for his father's clan. He is also related to his father's father's clan. There are other clan relationships that carry the same kind of relationships as the primary clan. When Navajos meet, they identify themselves by the clans to

Horned toad, good friend of the Code Talkers

which they belong. This is more important than one's name. All of these relatives are always brothers and sisters and have all the rights and privileges of the relationship. As one young Navajo said to me, realizing I was an Anglo when he spoke about his 'grandmother,' "Oh, she is not my grandmother in your understanding." The use of clan names became a very important part of the Navajo Code in World War II.

One aspect of the Navajo way of life most difficult for Anglos to understand is the mythical part of Navajo beliefs. Every Indian child was, and for the most part still is, taught the Navajo Way. These stories are explanations of why the Navajos are where they are today and why their world is as it is. This is a history based on Navajo myths that, in turn, give the ethical, moral and spiritual mores to The People.

These stories have been handed down through many generations. While the myths may differ in detail, depending on the storyteller, they are nevertheless sacred stories.

One story tells about the *horned toad* whose habitat is North America, ranging from Canada to Guatemala and from Kansas to the West Coast. He is a familiar figure to Navajos as they relate some of their myths and legends. According to Code Talker Albert Smith, the *horned toad* is known for the transmission of good messages. He might even be called the "mascot" of the Code Talkers who also were known for their good and accurate messages.

In his book, *Ma'ii and Cousin Horned Toad*, Shonto Begay notes that "Whenever we come upon a *horned toad*, we gently place it over our heart and greet it: 'Ya ateeh shi chi' ('Hello, my grandfather'). We believe it gives strength of heart and mind. We never harm our grandfather."[7]

Eighty-year-old Howard Gorman, a former tribal vice-chairman and elder statesman of the tribe, led me through his version of the *Navajo Way*.[8] First, according to Gorman, there was a Black World inhabited by spirits and Holy People. This First World was a misty place without much form or shape, but out of this mist First Man and First Woman were formed. These were Beings or Spirits that were not like the humans of today. In addition, there were many insect beings in this First World. Some of these Beings were evil.

Eventually, an opening appeared in this First World and the Beings, including the evil ones, floated up to the Second World. In this world, the Blue World, there were larger insects. There were also many different houses or rooms where animals lived. There was much quarreling and evil among the Beings there. It took First Man a long time to figure a way out of this world. Finally, by devising a special wand, the Beings were able to walk upward to the next world, the Yellow World. In this world there was no sun, but there were six mountains. Still, the Beings had little form or shape. Gradually, these Spirits would change into shapes. Slowly the shapes became more and more as we know them today. As they developed, but while they were still Spirits, they were given names like Squirrel, Deer, Spider and, of course, Coyote.

Coyote figures in many of the stories and legends of the Navajos. He is both tricky and secretive and, sometimes, downright evil. He was the one that stole the Water Monster's baby and caused a great flood in the Third World. First Man found out there would be a flood from the other animals and he told the Beings to come to the mountain. Howard Gorman likened this legend to the story of Noah and the Ark in the Old Testament. The Beings tried desperately to climb away from the flood and into the Fourth World. No tree would reach the sky. Finally, a female reed was planted. This grew rapidly and did reach the sky. The Beings could walk inside the reed on a spiral path until they reached the Fourth World.

In the Fourth World, First Man and First Woman now formed the four sacred mountains. They are Mt. Blanco in the East, Mt. Taylor in the South, the San Francisco Peaks in the West, and Mt. Hesperus in the North. Today these mountains form the boundaries of the Navajo Nation: the largest of our American Indian reservations: 16 million acres with approximately 200,000 inhabitants. One of the Beings was assigned to each of these mountains. Today these mountains remain sacred.

After entry into the Fourth World, the Beings made arrangements for the people to live in the world. They made a light, the Sun, for day, and a weaker light, the moon, for night. That trickster, the Coyote, was given the job of putting the stars in correct order. He did well with the Big Dipper, the Little Dipper, the North Star and the Seven Sisters. Soon he tired of his tedious and time-consuming job. Then he just tossed the remaining stars in the sky, and as Howard Gorman said, that is the reason they are up there so haphazardly.

Other decisions were made in this Fourth World. The seasons of the year were determined. Various kinds of corn—white, yellow, gray, blue, black and red—were made along with the seeds of other plants.

Unfortunately, all did not go well. Some poisonous powder, evil, had been sprinkled around, giving humans a choice as to whether to follow a good or a bad path. First Woman was discovered by First Man in the sin of adultery. Consequently, First Man and other male leaders decided to separate themselves from the females. This did not work for very long. The women became lazy about planting and became hungry. The men, who were lustful, decided the women were necessary. So, after cleansing and purifying ceremonies for both men and women were performed, they got back together. Into this picture comes Changing Woman called Mother Earth by some Anglos. She represents the four seasons, hence the name, "Changing. " (For further information, refer to

Wedding Basket. Note the opening is always to the East as it is with the door of the hogan. It is in the East the Sun rises, and prayers are said to God.

Navajo Myths, page 25.) We have discussed her previously as the mother of the Twins. After her Twins performed their assigned duties, and she approached the winter of her life, she went to dwell with the Sun. He built her a home in the Western Ocean where she lives today.

In addition to these mythical stories, ceremonies are also a very important part of Navajo life. Besides social dances, there are ceremonies for marking the entrance of a girl into womanhood, for blessing the *hogan* and for marriage, among others. In prehistoric days the Holy People were very close to the humans. From that time on, the correct way to perform all of these ceremonies has been handed down from generation to generation. It is important to perform each ceremony correctly or else it will not be effective and the Spirits will be angry.

Medicine men also figure prominently in the Navajo's life. Joe Perry, a Navajo employee for the gas company, spoke to me about medicine men.[9] Before a medicine man is called, a diagnosis of the illness is made. This is done by the Trembling Hand Man or the Star Gazer. The Trembling Hand Man can tell where the problem is by the way his hand shakes when it is over the ailing spot. The Star Gazer can tell by looking at the heavens. In either case, they can then tell the family which medicine man to call. Just like the Anglo doctor they have their specialties.

The total ceremony, performed under the leadership of the medicine man, is done for protection or for purification. It may take place over several days and nights, and involves singing, dancing, prayers, a gathering of many relatives and friends and the beautiful art of sandpainting.[10]

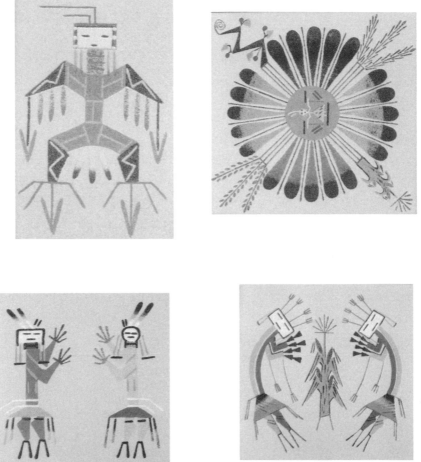

Isaac Wood Dugan

Sandpaintings are used in healing ceremonies. Pictured here are excerpts from larger paintings that represent Thunderbird, Sun and Eagle and sacred plants, Healing God, Double Rainbow and Corn.

The art of sandpainting is exacting, meticulous and painstaking work. A bit of sand of the proper color is held between the first two fingers. It is then pressed by the thumb to the specific point on the floor of the hogan to paint the picture. Simple! No indeed! It takes years of training to learn where to get the vegetation for the colors, then to color the sand, to learn the correct picture to paint for each ceremony, and finally to determine how to do the actual painting.

The sandpainting is done on the ground (but within the confines of the *hogan*) by several painters under the close supervision of the medicine man. The ceremony is usually done without any observers present.

During the ceremony, the person or patient for whom the ceremony is being performed will move to the center of the painting. Sand from the painting is then pressed on his body. This allows the cleansing spirits of the god, present in the painting, to enter the body of the patient. In this manner, the painting is destroyed in accordance with the instructions from the Holy People:

> *We will not give you this picture;*
> *men are not always as good as we;*
> *they might quarrel over the picture and tear it*
> *and that would bring misfortune;*
> *the black cloud would not come again,*
> *and the rain would not fall;*
> *the corn would not grow.*
> *But you may print it on the ground*
> *with the colors of the earth. . .*[11]

These beliefs–the *Navajo Way*–were familiar to all of the Code Talkers.

All of them were in good physical shape: the years of growing up on the Reservation had made them strong and adaptable to the hardships of nature.

Even though many had not completed high school, they were above average in intelligence. They all knew both the Navajo and English languages. They were able to understand the workings of the walkie-talkies and radios they'd be using in the field. Far and above all else, they had the moral stamina to withstand the tortures of an enemy determined to break the Code.

Despite these exceptional traits of the Code Talkers, questions remained: Why did the Code work so well? Why was it never broken? Code Talker Sidney Bedoni says that a code in English would have been broken immediately. When he was told that in Europe other language codes had been used, Bedoni's reply was: "Yeah, that's why they mostly got slaughtered. They should have started this program (the Code Talkers' program) right from the start. . . that way they wouldn't have had any trouble in Europe." Somewhat of an exaggeration, but Sidney Bedoni knew how important these Navajo coded messages were, and my curiosity continued. I needed to know how this Code was put together, why it worked so well, and why it was never broken.

Notes on Chapter II

1.   Mary Gorman's notes to the author reveal interesting facts on *hogans* including the Navajo spelling: *"hoghan"*.
2.   Words and music to the song are found in Appendix B.

The author is indebted to Dover Publications for granting permission to reprint "All Is Beautiful" from *The Indian Book* © by Natalie Curtis, Editor and Recorder, published by Dover Publications, New York, 1968.

2.   An informal conversation and visit with Shonto Begay was held in September, 1987.

3.   Informal interview in Ganado, Arizona, February, 1980.

4.   Witherspoon, Gary, *Navajo Kinship and Marriage* (Chicago and London: University of Chicago Press, 1975), pp. 33, 34.

5.   For further information see:

Between Sacred Mountains (Tucson: Sun Tracks and the University of Arizona Press, 1984), p. 148ff.

6.   Telephone interview in Phoenix, Arizona, 14 February 1980.

7.   Begay, Shonto, *Ma'ii and Cousin Toad* (New York: Scholastic, Inc., 1992).

8.   Personal interview with Grace and Howard Gorman, Ganado, Arizona, 3 February 1980.

Howard and Grace Gorman are fine examples of acculturation. Although a Christian, Howard tells of the *Navajo Way* with the same joy and belief as the Christian relating the Old Testament Bible Stories. He sometimes relates one to the other as in the case of the flood in the Third World and Noah's Ark in the Bible. He lives in a small house, not a *hogan*. The house is full of keepsakes. The mantle above the fireplace boasts an old Navajo wedding basket (see illustration, p. 31). When I asked if it had been used in his wedding, he said it had not been used for this purpose because he had a Christian ceremony; but others of his wife's family had used it. Grace showed me a medicine man's pouch with pollen still in it. Although the Gormans would not use it, it was, nevertheless, a prized possession. Grace told me of a dam which when built had destroyed some holy ground. Her brother, a medicine man, had predicted the dam would fail. Lately some seepage of water had occurred, and Grace wondered whether to relate this to the prediction or not. We speculated that the crack would be found and all would be well, but I could see that Grace still had some doubts. Grace and Howard lived in two worlds, accepting their beliefs from both, and living in peace and harmony with those who believed differently.

In January 1988 Howard Gorman died after losing a leg and fighting a gallant battle with diabetes. His funeral was one of the largest ever held on the Reservation. The then Navajo chairman Peter MacDonald spoke. MacDonald's most recent opponent, Peterson Zah, was also in attendance. The over-three-hour service was Protestant (Presbyterian) and spoken in both Navajo and English. It accentuated Howard Gorman's long and distinguished career on behalf of the Navajos he loved and respected.

9. Informal conversation in Ganado, Arizona, 3 February 1980.

10. For further information on the art of sandpainting, see: Eugene Baatsoslanii Joe, Mark Bahti, and Oscar T. Branson, *Navajo Sandpainting Art* (Tucson: Treasure Chest Publications, Inc., 1978); Frances J. Newcomb and Gladys A. Reichard, *Sandpainting of the Navajo Shooting Chant* (New York: J. J. Augustin, 1937, Dover ed., 1975); and Gladys A. Reichard, *Navajo Medicine Men Sandpaintings* (New York: J. J. Augustin, 1939, Dover ed., 1977).

11. Eugene Baatsoslanii Joe, Mark Bahti, and Oscar T. Branson, *Navajo Sandpainting Art* (Tucson: Treasure Chest Publications, Inc., 1978), p. 3.

The Code Talkers usually worked in pairs, two men behind or near enemy lines, the other pair at headquarters. These pictures show Code Talkers at work.

CHAPTER III

The Language and The Code

VERBAL COMMUNICATION has always been important to Native Americans. The Plains Indians, for instance, used message sticks as mnemonic devices. The message to be delivered was outlined by a series of notches on a stick. If the messenger was caught, no one could decipher the contents of the message. Smoke signals were also used by many tribes as an instrument of communication. Thus the sending and receiving of messages was viewed as important to successful warfare as were guns.

Although words are of great importance to the Navajo, they talk sparingly, often appearing to the non-Navajo as reticent. The "art" of conversation, the polite nuances, and the cocktail chatter of the Anglo are almost unknown to the Navajo. Children are not taught to say "please" and "thank-you," as are Anglo children. If a child asks for a drink of water, he is asking because the water is needed and it is not necessary to beg by saying "please." When he enters the Anglo world, he is often considered impolite and even rude until he learns the Anglo way. The beautiful Navajo poetry in Chapter II comes as a result of observation, of using words carefully and with precise meanings. The importance of word power to the Navajo was a major contributing factor to the success of the Code and the Code Talkers. Their language permits them to use words with great precision. Therefore, they were well suited to this war of words: a battle concept unknown to the Anglo soldier, who believed "actions speak louder than words."

Navajo was not the first Indian language to be used as a code in war. The code and cipher makers of World War I realized that Native Americans, with their little-known and unusual languages, might offer a distinct advantage in wartime.

On December 13, 1940, *The New York Times* reported that the Comanches, whose language was unwritten and little known at the time, were successful in confusing the Germans in the First

World War. Professor W. G. Becker, an authority on the Comanches from southwestern Oklahoma, said:

> One would be at a telephone at the front communicating with another back at headquarters. They would relay orders in their native language. The Germans had tapped the wires, and it must have driven them crazy.[1]

The earliest known use of an Indian language as a code came during World War I. As early as 1918, eight Choctaws were enlisted in the service with the 141st Infantry, Company D.

Apparently the American Expeditionary Forces also used Indian languages from tribes in Michigan and Wisconsin with some limited success.

The idea of using cryptography in World War I was the brainchild of Captain E. W. Horner, according to David Kahn.[2] These Indian languages and their use as cipher devices were not lost on the Germans after World War I. Determined to learn these languages, they sent "students" to the various reservations. Under the guise of studying other disciplines, they were actually learning the native languages with but one exception: the Navajo language.

The Germans may have also tried to infiltrate the Navajo tribe but with apparently little success. Code Talker John Benally remembers that during 1935 and 1936 while he was in school in Santa Fe, a foreigner befriended him. The stranger said he was studying the Navajo language and asked for Benally's help. Benally was glad to help and did so with pronunciation and vocabulary. He remembers thinking the foreigner was German and that he was probably going back to his country. Benally had no idea why the man wanted to learn the Navajo language. We can only speculate that he may have had orders from his government.

Shortly before the United States became involved in World War II, four Indians from Michigan and thirteen from Wisconsin were sent to the Louisiana war games to test their languages as a code using radio communication. A *New York Times* article on August 31, 1941, reported that it was most difficult to find Indians who still knew their tribal tongue and would not have difficulty translating it into English. *The New York Times* does not report how successful the Indian languages were during these war games. However, we can assume they did not perform as hoped. At that time their languages were abandoned as a tool for use in World War II.

By far, the most successful of the Indian language-usage codes has been the one used by the Navajo Code Talkers in the Pacific theater of World War II. It is the only code (language or otherwise) that has never been broken by the enemy.

The Code itself was worked out by the Navajos, but the original idea came from an Anglo named Philip Johnston. (The full text of Johnston's original proposal is reprinted in Appendix A.) Johnston, born in 1892, was the son of a missionary who lived on the Navajo Reservation. Young Philip became proficient in the Navajo language at an early age. When he was only nine years old, he and his father went to Washington with two Indian leaders to plead with President Roosevelt for land the Navajos had been living on. Philip acted as interpreter for this meeting.[3]

A few years later, Philip was still living on the Reservation. He was not only thinking in Navajo but also thought of himself as a Navajo. He attended college at the University of California, Los Angeles, graduated with a degree in civil engineering and fought in World War I.[4]

Following Pearl Harbor, his idea for a Navajo code was approved for a pilot project. Under a special dispensation (since he was overage) Johnston became a Staff Sergeant of the Marine Corps from 1942 to 1944. Along with four Navajos, Johnston developed the Code further while helping to recruit and train Code Talkers. Eventually, three to four hundred Talkers learned and used the Code. In 1970, shortly before his death, Philip Johnston was interviewed by John D. Sylvester for the Doris Duke Oral History Project and the University of Utah library. In his own words, Johnston tells the dramatic story of how the Navajo Code and the Code Talkers began:

> One day a newspaper caught my eye. An armored division on practice maneuvers in Louisiana had tried out a unique idea for secret communication. Among the

enlisted personnel were several Indians from one tribe. Their language might offer a solution for the oldest problem in military operations–sending a message that no enemy could possibly understand. The next day I confronted Lieutenant Colonel James E. Jones, area signal officer at Camp Elliott, seven miles north of San Diego. "Colonel," I asked, "what would you think of a device that would assure you of complete secrecy when you send or receive messages on the battlefield?" For a moment, the Colonel was silent. Dark circles under his eyes told their story of the strain under which he had been working. Why, he was plainly thinking, would gate guards permit a crackpot to enter this compound merely to waste my time?

With a deep sigh he leaned forward on his desk and answered my question: "In all the history of warfare, that has never been done. No code, no cipher is completely secure from enemy interception. We change our codes frequently for this reason." "But suppose we could develop a code from an Indian language," I continued, "one that would always be used orally, by radio or telephone, and never reduced to writing that would fall into the enemies' hands." "It has already been tried but with limited success. In World War I, Canadian forces attempted to use an Indian language when their telephone lines were tapped by the Germans. Trouble was that the Indians had no words in their vocabulary that were exact equivalents for military terms. For example, they could find no way of transmitting machine gun barrage. Let me remind you that any deviation whatever from the text of a message could lead to disaster. No, Mr. Johnston, I don't think your idea is practical."

"Ah, Colonel," I answered, "I'm afraid you're missing the whole point. My plan is not to use translations of an Indian language, but to build up a code of Indian words. Let's imagine this code included such terms as 'fast-shooter' to designate a machine gun, and 'iron-rain' for a barrage. Navajo personnel would be thoroughly drilled to understand and use these substitutions." A thoughtful expression crept into the Colonel's face. I pressed my advantage and went on. "Now just listen to some Navajo words and tell me if you honestly believe that anyone but a Navajo could understand them."

If I had lighted a string of firecrackers and laid them on the desk, the effect could not have been more startling. Colonel Jones set bolt upright in his chair and gazed at me in frank disbelief that such sounds could possibly issue from any vocal organ. . . Like a boxer who has his opponent reeling, I tried for a knockout. "I'll repeat one of them very slowly, and you try to pronounce it." After a painful and utterly futile attempt to do so, the Colonel roared with laughter. Recovering his composure he said, "Damn it, Mr. Johnston, you may have something there. I'd like very much to see some of these Navajos. Could that be arranged?"

After two weeks of searching Los Angeles for educated tribesmen, I returned with them to Camp Elliott. Colonel Jones greeted me with a broad smile. "We're all ready for you," he said, "a field telephone has been installed in Headquarters building. Here are six typical messages used in operations. See what your men can do, and, ah, report to me in an hour." At the appointed time we appeared at the Colonel's office and he guided us to the headquarters of Major General Clayton B. Vogel. It was a tense moment, but the General quickly put us at ease with a cordial greeting.

The room was swarming with high brass. Two of the Navajos were taken to another room and the test started. Fifteen minutes later, the General inspected the results. "These are excellent translations," he said, "as good as might be possible from any language. There's no doubt in my mind that Navajo words could be used for code purposes. I shall request the Commandant to authorize such a project immediately."

As Johnston and the Navajos tried to put the Code into effect, they were confronted with many problems. There were many military committees to go through. Many people wished to add their "expertise" to the project. Colonel Oliver P. Smith (who later became Commanding General of the 1st Division in Korea) said it sounded like an interesting program. He wondered what would happen to him when he was being court-martialed and he tried to explain to the court-martial board, "Well, my Indian Talker told me to attack."

In the beginning, it was assumed that at least a tenth grade education would be necessary in order to spell such words as artillery, bivouac, reconnaissance and strafing accurately. Later, it was found that some Navajos, despite very little formal education, could learn the Code correctly and use it effectively.

When William McCabe arrived at Camp Elliott with several other Navajos who had been recruited for "special training", no one was there to start the training. Johnston's commission had been delayed. McCabe tells of the rather rocky but impressive beginnings of the Code:

> We got there [Camp Elliott], there was nobody to lead us. No-body. . . to give us training. And I was the only one that had some college training so the captain integrated everybody. And finally they come out by elimination method that I was the one qualified to take over. So I took over. So they gave me thirty minutes to think something up or else call the whole thing off. . . 'cause there was nobody to tell us what to do. So we. . . name[d] all the services like the Army, and division and companies and battalions, regiments. . . instead of giving them regiments, regimental interpretations into Navajo, which would take a long time. And if you want to interpret "division" every time division comes up, why you'll have to interpret the whole thing. . . all of what it means. So instead of doing it that way. . . we just gave them clan names. . . Like "division" is named after the Salt Clan.
>
> . . .The idea is that we better use something that we're familiar with. We better not memorize anything else that we don't know. We already know what clan is... They can learn faster by using their own, the ones who they already know, they might think that their mother was this and their father was this, you know. And that way they think

the code after their mother was this or their grandpa or something. Then we got through with that. It took us all day long. And the airplanes, we name them after birds. And like the buzzard is the bomber and the hawk is a dive bomber and the patrol plane is a crow, and the humming-bird is the fighter.

. . . Artillery pieces we name after the pieces that we knew on this side–on Reservation. . . we already have guns. . . we didn't name those pieces secretly, we just name them outright. It's not important about the weapon. But what's important is planes and the men and all the stuff that's involved there appear to me was top secret. . . Airplane, why, if they know what, if it's a fighter or bomber or transport, well, they figure it out right now what it's meant for. Code names for the ships [of the Navy] we name them all after fish.

I imagine we just named the services one day and the alphabet the first day. . .We made the alphabet in which a boy by the name of Wilsie Bitsie. . . and Oscar Ilthma, he was half German. . . his father, I think, went to the First World War and he told us how they did it on the First World War–on the alphabet. So we use that one that they use in the First World War. But with different names– Navajo names. And we did all this for about a week and then we have to give them correct Navajo names–on spelling. That was twenty-six. . . seven. . . thirty years ago I was talking about. Golly. Well, in Navajo everything is in memory. . . from the songs, prayers, everything . . . it's all in memory. . . that's the way we were raised up.

. . . But we got everything down pat and then we still hadn't tried it on the telephone. And after a week or two, we practiced, we memorized. . . I grade papers, giving guys grades. . . And the guys that make the low grade, well, we keep them separate. And all the guys that have the higher grade we keep them separate and then when we send codes we put them up against each other. And I can see something that the slower. . . men would try to tell some-thing to the faster man and the faster man. . . says, "Come on. Hurry, hurry." That's how I got the idea that it would be better that way than to try to keep the slow guys together. Because when you get a fast guy and a slow guy up against each other, the slow one's always trying to do his best to come up. And at the same time the faster one is trying to pull him up.

. . . When we made that code. . . code within a code. . . the message comes out word for word on the other end, and including the semicolons, commas, periods, question marks, everything. We get all those.

And so was born the only code[5] the enemy was never able to decipher. There were many reasons for this. The inaccessibility of the language and the remoteness of the Reservation played a large part in the success of the Code. Linguists believe that as many as 200 languages existed in the North American continent when the Europeans arrived on the scene. These languages appeared to be unrelated to one another. All, except the Mayan, were unwritten at that time. Other than the Athabascans, who occupied large parts of northern Canada and much of Alaska, the Navajo/Apache tribe was the only one to have used the Athabascan root as their tribal language. Thus, it was a little-known and little-used language. The remoteness of the Reservation and the Navajo custom of living in extended families rather than communities constituted another reason for the success of the Code.

World War II is considered by many a "coming out" of the Navajo people into the world. Until that time life on the Reservation went on as it had for centuries. Families passed on the beliefs and tenets of the *Navajo Way* to their children. The children stayed on the Reservation and took up the tasks of living as had their parents and grandparents. The language that the child learned in the *hogan* was almost unknown among Anglos. Because it was so different to the Anglo ear, no one except for a few traders and missionaries bothered to learn Navajo. The traders who did learn some of the language were not really adept at conversing in Navajo about anything other than trading. Only a very few Anglos, of which Philip Johnston was one, knew the language in any depth. Except for the few isolated efforts by the Germans (see page 38), the potential enemy probably never considered the Navajo language important enough–or its people intelligent enough–to have developed a code based on their language.

As with many Indian languages, Navajo was not written until recently, although study of it was begun as early as 1852. A Franciscan, Fr. Berard Haile, was invaluable in these studies and in 1929 published his *Manual of Navajo Grammar*. It took World War II, however, for there to be a demand for a written dictionary of the language. The idea that culture, above a mere primitive existence, is possible without a written language, is difficult for many Anglos to understand. It is, no doubt, one of the major reasons why the White Man of the eighteenth and nineteenth centuries considered the Indian a savage. Even today (and certainly at the beginning of World War II) this feeling persists. The Navajos had no written constitution, no written treaties except those in Spanish or English, no written Bible or religious tenets, no written description of their arts or crafts and no written philosophies. That is why it is so difficult for the Anglo, who is proud of his writings, to conceive of a civilized culture without a written word. The spoken word–the passing from one generation to another of beliefs, actions and deeds–brought about a moral and civil society among the Navajos, a society at one with its surroundings and at one with the universe.

The English and Navajo languages differ greatly. In addition to the remoteness of the Reservation and the inaccessibility of the language, the Navajo language presents strange and unusual sounds for Anglos. Many other languages, including other Indian languages, can be pronounced sloppily and can still be understood. Not so with Navajo. When confronting the basic instructions for pronouncing vowels and consonants, the subtleties and complexities of this language become obvious.

To make vowel sounds even more complicated, there are both falling and rising tones contained in one word. Consonants often contain a glottal stop (sound is a stop and then a release much like the English expression "oh, oh").[6]

To pronounce the four basic vowels, a, e, i, o, of the Navajo language, one has to notice carefully the marks or lack of marks in the written version of Navajo.

There are many ways of sounding vowels, such as in the following chart for instance:

a – short and low in pitch
aa – long and low in pitch
á – a rise in pitch and short
áá – a rise in pitch and long
á – short, high and nasal
a – short and nasal
áá – long, high and nasal
aa ʼ– long and nasal
áa ʼ– falling tone
áa – falling nasal

One can say quite different things depending on the sound and the pitch given. Kluckhohn and Leighton[7] give some examples:

> A small clutch of the breath "glottal closure," which the speaker of European languages scarcely notices, often differentiates Navajo words. *Tsin* means "log", "stick", or "tree" whereas *ts'in* (the 'representing glottal closure) means "bone". Similarly, *bita* means "between" but *bit'a'* means "its wing."
>
> The words *bito'* (his water) and *bitoo'* (its juices) are absolutely identical save for the fact that the second vowel in the latter is lingered over.

The subtle difference in the Navajo words, "believer" and "alcoholic," hardly noticeable to the Anglo ear, is quite apparent to the Navajo ear. The two words caused one Anglo minister considerable difficulty as he spoke in Navajo in a small church on the Reservation. He inadvertently welcomed all the "alcoholics" to the service. He couldn't understand the muffled laughter among the usually reserved Navajo congregation until he was later told of his error. It is indeed small wonder that Lieutenant Colonel Jones stared in disbelief when he heard the Navajo sounds emanating from Philip Johnston.

After Marine Corps basic training, recruits were sent to the school to learn over 500 Navajo words which represented English words. The training was tough. It was necessary to learn every word and its meaning by rote. No Code Talkers would have the time or opportunity to consult a paper while under fire, and a paper could easily be stolen. For most Code Talkers this was the least difficult part of training. For centuries the stories and legends of the *Navajo Way* had been handed down by word of mouth. They were memorized by the children and, in turn, passed on to the next generation. The Code Talkers were learning and memorizing, too, as they grew up.

In addition, the Talkers needed to know the Morse Code in case it had to be used. In some cases semaphore flags and blinkers were used. Furthermore, they had to understand something of the workings of the equipment they would be using and how to set it up under less than ideal conditions. They also had to know how to survive in jungle conditions and behind enemy lines. The recruits often found themselves working in the field during the day and learning the Code well into the night.

Some code words would have the same literal meaning as the word being communicated. For instance:

Word	Navajo	Literal Translation
address	*yi-chin-ha-tse*	address
also	*eh-do*	also
appear	*ye-ka-ha-ya*	appear
native	*ka-ha-teni*	native
direct	*ah-ji-go*	direct

Such words would already be known unless the Navajo came from a section of the Reservation that used a different dialect. In these cases the pronunciation of the words taught by Johnston would have to be learned. In most cases, the English meaning of a word would be created from another Navajo word or combination of

Sarbo

Footprints through the stones of time. Communication by foot, by hand signals, by electronics and now talking. The Code Talkers show us the way.

Navajo words. The familiarity of the Navajos with nature led to many animal names being used. A dive bomber became a *chicken hawk* in recognition of the way the hawk finds its target. The *staring owl* was an observation plane. The *buzzard* circling in the sky looking for its prey was a bomber, while the little *hummingbird*, never lighting but always pricking the flower, was a fighter plane. Anyone on the Reservation knows how the eagle plucks its food and carries it through the air, so the *eagle* became a transport plane.

Descriptive phrases were used. Artillery was *many big guns*. An assault was a *first striker*. Assemble meant *to bunch together*. A bunker was a *sandy hollow*. A casualty was *to put out of action*. Coast guard was a *shore runner*. A dud was a *small dummy*, whereas a dummy was a *big dummy*. To entrench was *to make a ditch*. Whereas a fortification was a *cliff dwelling*, liaison was *to know other's action*.

Countries took on names with special meanings to the Navajos: Africa was known as *Blackies*. Alaska was *with winter*. America was *our mother* whereas South America was *south of our mother*. China became *braided hair* and Japan was *slant eye*. The relationship of Italy to *stutter* escapes me.

The Code is not without humor. Periodic becomes *period ice cat*. Bull dozer is *bull sleep*. Belong is *long bee*. Colon is *two spots*. Dispatch is *dog is patch*. And district is *deer ice strict*. Many of these words such as "periodic" represent a combination of the literal word and a spelling of the word.

If the enemy had ever deciphered the meanings of some of the words, and they apparently never did, the Code Talkers could suddenly switch to spelling out a word rather than using the code name. The Talker could do this by using A, B, C to tell his counterpart he was going to switch the code method, although it was not always necessary to first use A, B, C. By simply starting to spell by using the code words he had learned for the letters needed, he could switch the code method. Thus, it was possible to go back and forth, sometimes using code words for words or for letters.

To further add confusion, he could use *ant, apple,* axe for A; *badger, bear, or barrel* for B; and *cat, coal, or cow* for C. *Ant, badger, cow* could thus say "I am going to spell out the next word(s)." Instead of learning a 26-letter alphabet, the Code Talkers actually had to learn a 78-letter alphabet. When Mt. Suribachi on Iwo Jima was finally taken after a bloody battle and the American flag was raised, the message came through in Navajo: *Sheep, Uncle, Ram, Ice, Bear, Ant, Cat, Horse, Ice,* the first letters of the words spelling out, triumphantly, "Suribachi."[8]

(The last edition of the Code as used by the Talkers is located in Appendix C of this book.)

The Navajos are by their nature taciturn people to outsiders. Consequently, those who knew of the Code or of its development kept the secret well. One mistake was made; however, not by a Navajo. In a five-page article published in June 1943, in *Arizona Highways* magazine, James M. Stewart, then General Superintendent of the Navajo Indian Service reported:

> The U.S. Marine Corps has organized a special signal unit for combat communication service. A platoon of thirty Navajo was recruited in the Spring of 1942. Its members were trained in signal work using the Navajo language as a code, adapting a scheme tried with considerable success during World War I, when the enemy was completely baffled by the employment of an Indian language in front line communication.
>
> The thirty Navajo Marines performed their duties so successfully that the plan was expanded, a recruiting detail was sent back to the Navajo Reservation in the early autumn, and by early December, 67 new boys were enlisted. Two members of the original detachment went back as corporals to assist in explaining the work to eligible Indians. Corporals John A. Benally and John R. Manuelito have made good in the Marine Corps, a fact that anyone would guess at first sight. The boys look extremely competent. They are neat, poised, keen-eyed and fit. In movement and in manner they give the impression that they understand their business, the business of

making trouble for the enemy.

While the article was not completely accurate, it justifiably did upset the War Department. The entire project could have been compromised. Eventually, the War Department did believe the magazine's statement that it was an innocent mistake, and there was no further publicity about the project. It wasn't until twenty-five years after this incident that the Code Talkers were honored in an impressive ceremony and presented with a medallion for their outstanding service.

This secrecy and concern of the Navajos for their own Code Talkers was further emphasized by a young Indian who told me a story he had heard. Shortly after the war had ended, but before the code had been declassified, a Japanese-American agricultural expert was sent to the Reservation by the American government. He came to introduce a new hybrid of corn which, it was hoped, would produce more corn per acre. This man knew the Navajo language but was puzzled because no one would talk with him or be seen with him. He could get no one to discuss the new strain of corn. The Navajos were convinced he was a spy for the Japanese who wanted the code. His appearance and knowledge of the Navajo language became a decided deterrent when he was dealing with the protective Navajo families.

In addition to the uniqueness of the unwritten Navajo language, the remoteness of the Reservation and the abilities of the Code Talkers themselves, it was this Navajo commitment to keeping a major war secret that contributed to the success of the Navajo Code.

Notes on Chapter III

Some of the direct quotes in this chapter are taken from the Doris Duke Collection, as noted in the Introduction of this book.

1. *The New York Times*: "Comanches Again Called For Army Code Services," December 13, 1940, p. 16.
2. Kahn, David, *The Codebreakers* (London: Weidenfeld and Nicholson, New York: Macmillan, 1967), p. 549.
3. See Lagerquist, Syble, *Philip Johnston and the Navajo Code Talkers* (Council for Indian Education: Montana, 1983).
4. Ibid.
5. The late William McCabe's words were put on tape in 1971 for the Navajo Tribal Museum and the University of Utah. In 1992 Frank Thompson has a somewhat different version of the beginnings of the Code. In his words: "Code man William McCabe stated he had invented the Code. This statement is completely wrong. There were thirty of us who took training as communication men. I was the thirtieth man. To start with, we all trained in all type[s] and kinds of communication use–telephone, semaphore, blinker flags, walkie-talkies, larger size radio, Morse Code and finally putting Navajo words into Code. Philip Johnston did not develop the Code nor was he with us when we work[ed] out the Code (by the group of 30 men). All he did was suggest that the language be use[d] for communication."
6. For more information, see: Goossen, Irvy W. *Navajo Made Easier*, revised edition (Flagstaff: Northland Press, 1967, revised edition, 1975), pp. xiv, xv.
7. Kluckhohn, Clyde and Leighton, Dorothea, *The Navaho* (Cambridge, Massachusetts, and London: Harvard University Press, 1946, 1974, 3rd printing, 1979), p. 257.
8. While this is the usual translation of the message as it came through, some of the men who were on Iwo Jima remember the message as spelling out Mt. Scppa, not Suribachi.

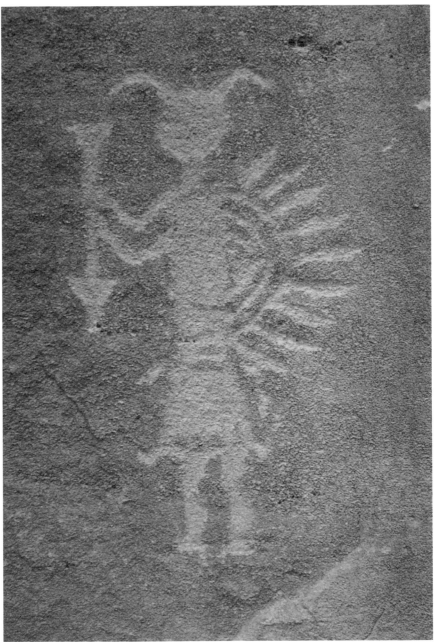

Stones of time reveal another ancient wayfarer, or perhaps a depiction of a "Holy Man.".

CHAPTER IV

From Boot Camp to Action,

1941–1946

In 1940 AND EARLY 1941, World War II was going well for the Axis powers in the European theater. Great Britain was the only Allied power still left fighting on the western front. France had fallen. Italy was part of the Axis. On the eastern front, the Soviet Union was valiantly trying to hold its own, but German forces were continuing to march through Europe. Leningrad and Stalingrad were in jeopardy. Japanese plans for the specific attack on Pearl Harbor had begun in the summer of 1941 even while Japanese and American diplomats were negotiating in Washington, DC.

When the United States refused to withdraw its oil embargo against Japan and demanded that the Japanese forces withdraw from China and Southeast Asia, Japan's Premier General Tojo Hideki decided to attack. While United States Secretary of War Henry Stimson wondered how Japan could be maneuvered into firing the first shot without too much damage, the bombing of Pearl Harbor came as a complete surprise to the majority of our citizens. The devastating loss of lives and property sent a chilling message to the residents of California who assumed they were next, as did the residents of the Navajo Nation.

On December 8, 1941, the United States Congress (with only one dissenting vote) declared war on Japan. Three days later Germany and Italy declared war on the United States. Congress, this time unanimously, declared war on these two Axis powers. Almost at once, Americans united behind the war effort.

Americans responded quickly to the December 7, 1941, attack on Pearl Harbor. Men and women, not waiting to be drafted, were ready to volunteer when recruitment offices opened on Monday morning, December 8. Many of those in the recruitment lines were Navajos. As noted in the first chapter of this book, the relationship between the Navajos and the Anglos had historically been one of mistreatment and neglect by the Anglos.Nevertheless, according to Code Talker R. O. Hawthorne, the Navajos had great respect for one of their own who entered the service.

To the Navajos, the attack on Pearl Harbor was as much an attack on the Navajo Nation as it was on the forty-eight states. Therefore, they felt they had to defend the beauty of their Reservation and its holy ground. This may seem inconsistent with the treatment the Navajos received at the hands of Kit Carson and General Carleton. However, it is not inconsistent with the Navajos' love of their land; nor with the belief of many older Navajos that it was the Utes and other warlike Indian mavericks who actually provoked the battle in Canyon de Chelly that led to the Long Walk.

Despite the problems of the Long Walk and its aftermath of starvation and poverty, the resilient Navajos had grown from a few thousand to over 40,000 in 1933. The people had prospered. Many families had over a thousand head of sheep and cattle. Navajo art in the form of rugs and silver had become well known.

The editors of *Between Sacred Mountains*[1] describe this as "The times old people remember now when they talk of the 'traditional life.' They were times when the land and the seasons told people how to live. When the land said, 'Take your stock to better grass,' the people moved. When the weather said, 'It's time to go to winter camp,' the people went. When the trees said, 'Now you will pick pinon nuts,' it was done."

In 1933 John Collier was head of the Bureau of Indian Affairs (BIA) in Washington, DC. He and his colleagues decided that Navajo land, as well as other western homelands, was being overgrazed. Navajo families were told that they must get rid of some of their animals. And the tribal council of the time agreed. While it was apparent that many animals were dying around them, livestock owners were reluctant to obey and some would hide their sheep, horses and cattle from federal regulators. Collier decided to enforce the stock reduction edict. Those families who would not sell off some of their livestock found, to their horror, that their horses, sheep and goats were shot and left to rot.

Grazing districts were formed, and finally grazing permits were issued. These permits are still required today. Whether or not stock reduction was necessary, the land never returned to its former state. This has been true in other countries where land has been overgrazed and not replenished. For the Navajos it meant the beginning of a gradual loss of old traditional ways. As one writer put it: "The land is unhappy." No longer were the land and the people inseparable.[2]

The stock reduction plan, as implemented in 1933 and 1937, came at a time when the future Code Talkers were impressionable–when they would have been looking to a future of sheepherding and carrying on the traditional Navajo life. In the years following the Long Walk, the Navajo had accepted a dependence on the federal government. And this was reinforced by the stock reduction program. So these young men were caught in a time of crumbling traditions and dependency on the federal government. When the Japanese attacked the United States, this very dependency and lack of a future on the Reservation helped to propel the young Navajo volunteers to the recruiting stations.

In the early twentieth century, birth records were usually not kept on the Reservation. Knowing one's exact birth date was a matter of memory and hearsay. So, it became easy for a man to lie about his age. With the armed services' immediate need for recruits, he could be accepted quickly, with few age verifications, by eager recruiters. Many of the Code Talkers were underage when they volunteered for the Marine Corps at recruitment stations set up on the Reservation. Some of those who reported for Army duty and demonstrated a knowledge of the Navajo language were asked to report as volunteers for a "new" Marine Corps program being organized. Many of them eventually became Code Talkers, while others were found in boot camps throughout California.

Dan Akee had to volunteer four times before he was accepted. Most of his friends had gone, and although he was underage, he wanted to go too. The first time he volunteered, his mother would not sign the papers. After going back to school and realizing that he probably didn't need proof of age, he volunteered again. This time he didn't pass the physical because of his eyesight. The third time he was rejected because he was flat-footed. The last time he volunteered, he was accepted. His flat feet were ignored this time, as recruiters realized he was usually barefoot on the Reservation and could outrun most other volunteers. Then, intending to ask for Navy duty, Akee mistakenly asked for the Marines, probably having heard about them from his friends. After boot camp, "they" told him he wanted to volunteer as a paratrooper. Another officer, however, told him it was more important to join the Code Talkers. "You can save many lives with your words, you know." So, he was sent to Camp Pendleton and became a Code Talker.

Albert Smith, past president of the Code Talkers' Association said he was first refused because he was only 15. After returning home for only a few days, he went back to the Recruiting Office, added two years to his age and was accepted.

As the Navajos volunteered for and were inducted into the Marine Corps, the first contact for many of them was with the autocratic personnel of the service. This may have made the acculturation process somewhat easier, because they were immediately part of a group of soldiers and no distinctions were made except those of rank. As with all draftees and volunteers, the men were given physical and mental tests. Those who passed were sent to basic training in San Diego.

Some of the Navajos went through the eight weeks of boot camp as the only Indian in their platoon. They found it extremely tough, not only because of the physical hardships and demanding tests, but also because of the cultural transition from the Reservation to the Anglo world. Those who were not away at school when they volunteered for duty were primarily sheepherders on the Reservation. Most had been raised in a *hogan* with the traditional Navajo family.

Others adjusted surprisingly well to being thrust suddenly into the Anglo culture. Before he volunteered, Paul Blatchford had been in charge of the BIA two-way radio operation on the Reservation. He was one of only a few who had experience with modern communication methods and modestly says he scored somewhat higher on the aptitude tests.

Away from the Reservation for the first time at the age of 15, Peter MacDonald remembers with awe the lights, signs, multitudes of people and the excitement of the city. He had been taught that the Navajo people were the only ones who mattered. They were the chosen ones. To see so many non-Indians who obviously also thought of themselves as important came as a complete surprise. The Code Talker had stepped out of the Navajo culture into an unknown world with unknown people in an unknown land to fight in a war he saw as necessary to preserve his homeland.

Thomas Begay, also underage, had never been in a motel, a hotel or on a train. From Santa Fe, he was given a ticket for a train to San Diego. Not knowing any better, he entered the freight part of the train. Eventually, he found his way to a sleeping car but wasn't aware that it provided sleeping space. So, he spent the entire night just sitting all the way to Los Angeles, lonely, forlorn and wondering what he had done to himself. Eating was another problem for Begay. He told about it this way:

> I was never used to that kind of stuff, you know just the Navajo food, you know . . . There was some butter I couldn't eat and some things I didn't like to eat. As I got to the end . . . before you have to put it away there was somebody standing there, saying "you eat it right now." I just swallowed it just like that without chewing . . . I would say, was pretty rough on us. You come from a hogan into this, all this. Where you've never been . . . It's a hard adjustment.

The Navajo man's long hair has always been symbolic. So getting a haircut, especially a World War II Marine-type haircut, was an experience most will never forget. Even today, adjusting to the contemporary Anglo haircut is still a problem for some Navajos.

Jimmy King found adjusting somewhat easier. He had the opportunity "to be out" and off the Reservation through his amateur boxing. He fought in Albuquerque and Denver and "was accustomed to all the excitement and noise." He even "had a little taste of fame." However, his somewhat easier adjustment to the Anglo world was atypical of most Navajos.

There were many misconceptions about Anglos among the Navajos. Few Navajos had much contact with the White Man, except for occasional tourists, and the traders. R. O. Hawthorne says he thought the White Man could do no wrong, that "he was upstanding, upright in everything he did." It was a real letdown to find out that they "were no different than we are." This reversed itself with the White Man. The Anglo expected the Navajo to be an expert archer, but the Navajo had not used bows and arrows for years. The Navajo's eyesight was not keener than that of his fellow Marine. In Hawthorne's words:

> Most people believed in the past that Indians . . . walked a straight line. And his word was truth . . . of course the white boys probably were taken aback to find out that this wasn't always the case . . . I was taken aback to find out, on the other hand, that it wasn't the case with them either.

Most Navajos have little need for shaving tools, but as part of the Marine Corps equipment all recruits were issued razors. Johnny Benally relates the story:

> One of our men had one or two whiskers and the sergeant came up and we had close-up inspection . . . he come up and look at this guy in the face and said, "Did you shave this morning?" . . . He says "No, sir." . . . "When did you shave last?" He answered back, "I have never shaved in my life."

Paul Blatchford tells of a lieutenant who was making everyone shave on the front lines. The Navajos said, "We can't do that. Indian custom. We cannot do that. Once you touch your beard or pull your hair, you die." Finally, the lieutenant said, "Is that true? Tomorrow I'll shave, we'll find out." Blatchford recounted, "So he did shave that morning. And at nine o'clock, he got shot right square in the forehead." Shaving was optional after that.

The misconceptions on both sides became a learning process for all. The Code Talkers became a part of Anglo society, but they did not leave behind the *Navajo Way*. They were constantly called "Chief" by their Anglo friends and officers. Even though there hadn't been a chief among them for years, the Navajos took the nickname in stride and came to respond to it in a friendly way. Early in the war, to his embarrassment, Carl Gorman responded quickly to a call on his ship for "the chief," only to discover that warrant officers were also known as "chief." "Who are you?" he was asked when he reported for orders. "I'm a Navajo chief," was the answer. To the officer's credit, he looked at Gorman and said, "He is the real chief."

The training of the Code Talkers was intense and arduous. While most Navajos were accustomed to taking orders from teachers and parents, most were not used to the discipline they found in the Marines. Life on the Reservation was free–free to roam the plateaus bringing in the sheep, free to talk or sit in silence with the family, free to eat when hungry and sleep when tired, free to indulge in the beauty of one's surroundings. Life in the service was not free, from the moment the bugler blew his wake-up call before sunrise, until nighttime, falling into a bed that had been made many times during the day to satisfy exacting requirements. This discipline, as difficult as it was, most Code Talkers say, was a very positive aspect of their training. Many agree with James Nahkai, Jr. who notes:

> . . . In the Marines . . . they teach you discipline. You either learn it or they kick you out. And this, I mean, this has helped me a lot. In any job I've been in I've learned that one phrase . . . If you want to give orders you've got to learn to take orders.

William McCabe echoes Nahkai, saying that the Marine Corps discipline was the one thing that helped him in later life.

For the Navajos who were in boarding school when they enlisted, the discipline was not as traumatic as it was for those who had come directly from the *hogan*. They learned some of the "niceties" of living in the Anglo world. They knew how to wash and iron their clothes. They marched to classes that made military drills easier. They could adjust to groups better than those who had lived the solitary life on the Reservation.

Because the strict, often cruel, school officials insisted on complete adherence to the English language and Anglo ways at all times, these boarding schools were not popular with most students or parents.

Boot camp did have its lighter moments, especially for those who were in mostly Navajo platoons. During training, one Anglo sergeant, having no knowledge of the complex way Navajos communicate even simple numbers, had the idea that the Navajo could count cadence in his native language. "Gee whiz," says William McCabe, "you had to take three, four steps before count[ing] one." The Navajos turned to laughter, started calling the sergeant names in Navajo, and the drill became a shambles. The sergeant no longer asked for cadences in the Navajo language.

After basic training at the Marine Corps Depot in San Diego, most Code Talkers went to Camp Elliott for further exercises. As the war progressed and the Code proved itself in the field, recruiting and training of the Code Talkers was accelerated. Alex Williams, Sr. went through basic training in four weeks instead of the usual eight. Wilfred Billey was with a group of 50 to 60 men in Code Talkers' school. Classes before 1943 had been much smaller. Among the instructors of these intensive courses were: John Benally, Jimmy King, Rex Kontz, Johnny Manuelito, and Ross Haskie.

Quite a few of the potential Code Talkers flunked out, sometimes from serious drinking. Alcoholism among Navajos became a problem when the cultures clashed. There were, of course, other contributing reasons for alcoholism. The young male Navajo brought up in the traditional matrilineal society found it difficult to prove his maleness in the Anglo-American male macho society.

The male on the Reservation was taught that drinking is a part of the pleasure of being with his clan peers. Once he stepped out of this group and into an unknown culture where the man is head of household, excessive drinking may have become a way for the Navajo to prove his masculinity to the Anglo society.

The Code Talkers also needed to demonstrate a high degree of moral character not found in all soldiers. Jimmy King, one of those responsible for selecting those who would become Code Talkers after training says:

> And there was character. Some of them [the recruits] misconduct themselves in boot camp, or else at some of the training schools. Have a weekend . . . and they end up in the jug. And then the following Monday morning there has to be a guard coming behind them with a rifle. And we didn't think we could trust that kind of people. We knew that [if] a man had a good character, you could trust that man. He wouldn't lie to you. He would lay his life down, just like we would . . . And we would make this very clear . . . I pounded this into everyone that went through my classes. And you think that you love your country well enough that you would lay your life down. Supposing you were captured tonight and they had a Sumari, just cutting inch by inch and making you tell what [a] word meant. . . . The minute you saw that blood begin to run, are you gonna tell? Of course not, you wouldn't. You'd give your life before you'd tell them. Are you devoted that much to the Marine Corps, to the country that you love, to your motherland? They'd say, "Yes." I didn't hear you. They'd say, "Yes." I didn't . . . quite hear you. Again—"YES!" Just like that. [If I didn't think he was qualified to join] I didn't have any hard feelings against . . . the man [if] his hair wasn't combed right, or else his shoe wasn't tied just so, but knowin' in my heart and back of my mind. I know that that man was not going to make it. He's going to foul up. He's going to cost hundreds, maybe even thousands of lives. I know it's better to leave him.

Other potential Code Talkers were found to be lacking much of the basic English vocabulary. Their knowledge of English and Navajo could not be superficial. Jimmy King tells why all Anglos, with the exception of Philip Johnston and some Navajos were eliminated from the program:

> We had a hard time with some of the white boys that thought they knew the Navajo language. . . . They were born out here on the trading posts. Their parents were Indian traders. And they were brought up among the Navajos, with the Navajos. They played with the Navajos during their childhood. They picked up the language so well, but never well enough that they could pass the tests to be one of the Code Talkers. They spoke the language like coffee, sugar, and flour and counting of money. They knew how to say that. But there also was always a fraction of a syllable that they could not pronounce exactly as well and precise as it should be so there would be no maybe and if about it . . . There were [some] words that they'd never heard. All they knew was what was known as trading-post language–trading with Indians, a pair of gloves, a pair of shoes–they knew that, all that, well. But they could not carry on a conversation outside of the Navajo trading post language. And we had to eliminate some of our own Navajo people.

Ability with languages came easily to the Code Talkers. Thomas H. Begay tells how easily he could learn languages:

> Most of my education was in the service. There . . . [were] a lot of courses that I took. I took Russian. I took Japanese. In fact, I was classified as an interpreter in Japanese. In fact I got my discharge papers "interpreter–Japanese." I was interpreter for the company.
>
> [There is some similarity between Japanese and Navajo languages], like *T'do-go-ya*, that means "barber shop" . . . in Navajo that means "go down the spring . . . down the wash . . . down the water." But it's very simple to learn Japanese–for me. It was easy. I could write it, read it, you

know, interpret. So I took Russian, but I couldn't get any-where so I quit.

Dan Akee describes the Code as a puzzle–a puzzle to be learned by the Navajos–but impossible to be learned by others lacking the same background.

A retentive memory was necessary, as was the ability to make quick changes under actual war conditions. "We learned things under fire," said Jimmy King, "under actual battle conditions. And we employed those new ways of sending messages quicker and faster. And we had to adopt new names–place names–because of change of geographical locations, different islands . . . Navy devised different ships, different weapons . . . So what you started off with we didn't do on Okinawa."

Tests were conducted with professional cryptographers, and the Code Talkers were found to have greater speed and accuracy in every case. In one such test Signal Corps officers ("a bunch of white-haired men," according to John Benally) had gathered to see if they could break the Code. They were working with tapes made at Camp Elliott while the Code Talkers were practicing. Apparently, they were unsuccessful. So, they called John Benally to Intelligence Headquarters to see if he could decode the practice messages. He immediately de-coded them correctly and was told to leave the room. He never found out whether the "old men" figured out the Code, but the supposition is that they did not. Another officer, when testing the Code Talkers, thought to trick them with many punctuation marks. He put in a comma, exclamation point, semicolon, question mark and even a star for further confusion. All were received and decoded perfectly.

In addition to learning the Code, the Code Talkers needed to be mechanical enough to understand radio equipment: how it worked, how to put it together and how to fix it in the field. Radio training was done with TBX equipment. After arrival overseas, most of the men were given a smaller walkie-talkie powered by batteries.

The story of how Johnston lost his first Navajo radio instructor to the Code Talkers (Anglo instructors had been used previously) is told by Paul Blatchford. Restless at his seemingly unimportant assignment, Blatchford learned the Code at night and begged to go overseas. Having been told by a "friend" that if he went "over the hill" (AWOL) he would automatically be assigned overseas when he returned, he left the base and hitchhiked as far as Flagstaff, Arizona. Flagstaff, just off the Reservation, was cold and miserable. Blatchford, now two days overdue, decided it was time to go back to the base.

Arriving in Oceanside, California at about three o'clock in the afternoon, he met, by chance, a group of women Marines who, being very curious about Indians, asked, "Hey, Chief, are you one of those Code Talkers?" There followed a friendly talk about life on the Reservation and ended with an invitation to ride back to the base with the women in their bus. Sitting amongst all the women he was not noticed by the guard at the gate and so allowed back on the base without any difficulty. Johnston, however, was angry at the absence of one of his good instructors and, correctly following orders, reported Blatchford to the colonel. The colonel, not believing Blatchford's story, tried to find what he called the "real story" of the Marine's absence.

Finally, after Blatchford had made up a story of his absence and re-entrance to the base, the colonel said he would not send Blatchford to the brig if he would just "volunteer" for the 5th Reconnaissance. Thus, Johnston lost his only Navajo radio instructor, and Blatchford and five other Navajos were shipped overseas, first to Hawaii and then to Iwo Jima. In two weeks, Blatchford was made a corporal: he was the senior member of the group.

For the most part, the Code Talker did his job with only one partner. He had to be adept at surviving behind enemy lines. In one training session Anglos and Navajos were led into the desert with only one canteen of water. The exercise was to see how long they could last on that amount of water. The Navajos knew very well that they could use the cactus plant for all the water they needed, but they didn't let the Anglos in on the secret. After ten days in the desert the Anglos, including the head of the project, had to be helped back to headquarters. The Navajos still had water in their canteens and showed no signs of weakness.

The Navajos were usually shorter in stature than the Anglos but they made up for this in strength. They were accustomed to the rugged life on the Reservation. Few of those selected as Code Talkers had any difficulty with the physical tests, except for swimming. On the Reservation not many Navajos had an opportunity to learn how to swim. The test was a simple one: each recruit was thrown in the water, sometimes blindfolded, and it was sink or swim. Eventually he would pop to the surface, and with his survival instinct, learn to swim the hard way. Raphael Yazzie was held for an extra month before going to Camp Pendleton because he couldn't pass the swimming exam. Another Code Talker had learned to swim in a pool near his home.

For most of the Code Talkers, Hawaii was the final training ground. Here, from the ships that would take them to the battle areas, they practiced the maneuvers involved in taking an island. These practice landings were made on several of the smaller islands. Code Talkers who had been in battle helped with the training, changing the code as necessary, giving warnings and precautions to those who were to go into battle for the first time.

When Thomas Begay was sent back to Hawaii from Iwo Jima, he was asked to review all of the messages sent there. In light of what he learned from this review, he was asked to stay in Hawaii to train other Navajos in communications at the Naval Fleet School. He also helped retrain Code Talkers who were brought there from many of the Pacific islands.

Hawaii also offered a final opportunity for recreation before entering the battle zone. Parker Ranch, a sprawling, popular resort on the big island of Hawaii, was often turned over to the military during the war. On one occasion a rodeo was planned. The rodeo became a common ground for the American Anglo and the American Indian, as all took part in the competition. However, the light-hearted fun at Parker Ranch quickly gave way to more sobering pursuits.

The normally benign tropical islands of the South Pacific were now the scene of grueling days and nights under heavy enemy artillery. Men often went for days without sleep and with only the infamous K-rations to sustain them. Except for the contacts with soldiers who had come back to Hawaii for rest and relaxation and the mute evidence of the attack on Pearl Harbor, the Code Talkers had little knowledge of what was ahead of them as they did their final training on the big island of Hawaii.

For most, Pearl Harbor was the embarkation point. Because they were sent to different platoons and battalions throughout the war zone, it's impossible to trace a typical Code Talker through his duty in the Pacific islands. Some saw fierce fighting on several islands. Some were assigned to clean-up squads. Some were wounded and sent back to Hawaii after only one battle. Others were wounded, patched up and sent immediately back into the war zone.

The Code Talkers' Association tells me that 25 Code Talkers who served with the 4th Marine Division joined, left, returned and were discharged with the main unit. Eight additional Code Talkers were assigned to this unit just before the end of the war. Obviously, this group was kept together throughout the war. Assignments were different for some of the other 300 to 400 Code Talkers who served.

Now, after all their training, both physical and mental, the Code Talkers were given their assignments. They would finally test their courage and ability under the strange and gruesome conditions of war in the Pacific islands.

Notes on Chapter IV

Some of the direct quotes in this chapter are taken from the Doris Duke Collection, as noted in the Introduction of this book.

1. Mitchell, Barney, *Between Sacred Mountains* (Tucson, Arizona: Sun Tracks and the University of Arizona Press: 1984), p. 155.
2. Ibid., p. 174.

From the National Archives comes this picture of two Code Talkers work-ing in the Pacific field of operation during World War II. Note the resem-blance to the Japanese as well as the bulky equipment that have to be transported.

CHAPTER V

Island by Island
Across the Pacific

AFTER THE SHOCK OF Pearl Harbor, the Japanese pressed their advantage in the Pacific. Island by island the enemy advanced. On Christmas Day in 1941 the British surrendered Hong Kong. On January 2, 1942, the Philippines fell; Singapore fell in February. After the fall of Corregidor in early 1942, the remaining United States troops under General Douglas MacArthur had retreated to Australia. It was not until the middle of 1942 and into 1943 that the tide began to turn.

United States forces started slowly to advance island by island toward the aggressor, Japan. General MacArthur in the southwestern Pacific and Admiral William F. Halsey, Jr. in the southern Pacific began the Allied conquest of the islands and moved towards Japan. As each island was secured, it was used for storing supplies and equipment. On some, airstrips were established from which bomber and fighter planes could be used to attack. Many of these islands, including Hawaii, Australia, and New Zealand, were used for rest, relaxation and retraining.

Since it became necessary to revise and enhance the Code during the war, many of the Talkers spent time retraining on these islands. They learned new words and phrases that had to be adapted to the Code. New and better techniques were also learned for sending and receiving their messages.

In his proposal for the establishment of the Code Talkers, Philip Johnston wrote that the "Navajos are in a unique position to render service in the defense of the United States, a service that will be of inestimable value." At that time, very few would have predicted just how valuable this service would become.

As the war in the South Pacific became an exercise in island-hopping, sending messages to and from the various islands was of paramount importance. When the United States forces landed on an island and fought to take possession, headquarters needed to know exactly what opposition they were meeting and where reinforcements were necessary.

Few examples of verbatim orders given and received in the field under fire have survived. The Marine Corps Manual Sample Operations Orders, used in the training of the Code Talkers, reveals some examples of messages sent and received:

Reached objective at 1945, reorganizing
Enemy riflemen under the protection of heavy artillery
support
Machine-gun fire on right flank
Continue to advance
Consolidate your position
Landing wave on beach, but losses high
Am forced to dig in
Right flank in danger–send reinforcements

Messages were used for supplies, for logistics and for operations:

Men low on rations
Men low on water
Need ammunition

When planes were spotted, messages were relayed in code to the front lines. Messages from the front lines to headquarters would tell where to drop bombs. Often front-line Code Talkers would function as front-line observers and would relay the movement of fire, the location, even the elevation. At times, messages were sent about the landing of troops: where, when, and how many. James Nahkai, Jr. and his partner, Lloyd Oliver, while stationed at headquarters would alert the battalions when a certain sector was to be hit. They also relayed the change of password to all the battalions each day.

Even in occupied Japan all messages about the atomic bomb devastation in Nagasaki, as well as the conditions in certain gun factories, were relayed by Navajo Code Talkers to San Francisco headquarters. According to Major Howard M. Conner, Signal Officer of the 5th Division on Iwo Jima, more than 900 messages were sent and received without an error. A plan had been devised by which messages could be repeated if it was thought there might be an error. However, as far as I could determine, this was used only in a few minor cases and never in any of the major messages.

In hundreds of life or death situations, the Code Talkers were able to save lives with their timely messages. Philip Johnston tells of meeting an Anglo Corporal at Camp Pendleton who said, "It might interest you to know that I consider these Navajos to have saved my life on one occasion." The Corporal was on Saipan facing the Japanese forces on the edge of a lake. During the night the enemy retreated and established a new position. The United States forces moved up to the old position of the Japanese. Immediately, shelling started from other United States forces. Frantically they called for a Code Talker who sent the message that the United States was bombarding its own men. The firing was immediately stopped. "And that is how the Navajo saved my life," explained the Corporal.

According to Vernon Langille,[1] one of the Anglo Marines who worked with the Code Talkers, the Navajo Code was "American double-talk mixed with a sound that resembles water being poured from a jug into a bathtub."

If this wasn't already confusing enough to the enemy, the Navajos were able to improvise, in the heat of battle, sending and receiving messages that included words not even included in the original code. This was possible because of the great care taken by the Navajos who first set up the code. By using the precise meanings of each Navajo word, in new combinations, and verbs that could be changed according to what one wanted to say, Code Talkers could create, and understand, messages using words not in the learned Code. And, they could send and receive these crucial messages with great speed and accuracy.

The Navajo Code was constantly being updated and revised as the men in the field found different uses for it. On Peleliu, every Code Talker was given two code numbers. If he should be captured and the Japanese asked him to send a message, he was to send the message with his code number inserted. Then headquarters would know that the message was not a legitimate one.

Even those who used Navajo as their native language could not understand the Talkers. The sad story is told of a Navajo–not a Code Talker–who was taken prisoner. By this time the Japanese knew the Navajo language was being used in code. They tortured the Navajo prisoner almost to death trying to make him reveal the Code. He could not have done so even if he had the desire. He knew only the Navajo language and not its use as a code.

Once they were thrown into the front lines of the bloody war, the Code Talkers faced many problems not related to their specialized training. One was their physical resemblance to the Orientals, as has often been noted by anthropologists who theorize that the Navajos came to North America across the Bering Strait.

R. O. Hawthorne says he remembers "many times that our own troops would capture some of the Navajo Code Talkers and take them in for interrogation because they thought we looked like the Japanese." Code Talker Sidney Bedoni says that he was always supposed to be with a White Man when he was behind enemy lines so that he could be identified as a Marine. William McCabe tells of his experiences on Guadalcanal while waiting on the beach for his transport ship to arrive:

> But something went wrong and we had to wait there for about four or five days before we could board the ship. And we hadn't been eating for a day, day and a half, something like that. And to do this, to eat we'd have to set up our mess hall again. We already broke the thing down . . . already packed. And we couldn't eat with the Army . . . they didn't want no Marines out there. So I went to the chow dump, and I was sneaking around back there and open up can, open up boxes. These guys that went with me took what they want. You know, they just took a can of meat or can of fruit or vegetable or something . . . what they want they took off and went off. But I got choosy, I wanted to get me a can of orange juice. Damn right. I wanted an orange juice. So then that, I got lost among the

big chow dump and I got caught back there. All of a sudden somebody says, "Halt," and I kept walking. "Hey, you! Halt, or I'm gonna shoot!" And I thought somebody was playing a joke on me. I turn around and there was a big rifle all cocked and ready to shoot. And so, "What are you doing here?" I said, tell him "I'm just from my outfit. I was coming here to get something to eat." And he said, "I think you're a Jap. Just come with me."

Finally, after more threats, William McCabe was identified and released, but after this incident the Marines ordered:

one of the boys . . . one of the white guys to guard me. Everywhere I went he went, everywhere I went he was there. I went down to the toilet, he was there. I went down to take a bath, he was down there. He was everywhere. He'd go to sleep and I'd start walking and he'd say "Where are you going?" "I don't give a damn. You just come follow me."

National Archives

And he had to follow me everywhere I went. He tried to tell me to stay in one place, but I'd roam all over. "He goes again. There he goes again. Damn Chief, why don't you sit still, stay put? My legs are hurting." And then we went on ship. It was in the Australian paper when we got there. Somebody put it in the newspaper.

In addition to the physical resemblance of the Navajo to the Oriental, the language also seems to have a certain similarity. Other American soldiers, not familiar with the Code Talkers and thinking they were hearing the Japanese language, sometimes tried to jam the frequencies upon which the Navajos were sending and receiving messages.

The Navajo fear of the dead made the horrible conditions of war even more chilling to those Code Talkers who believed and practiced the *Navajo Way*. The fear of the dead involves ghosts. Ghosts are the evil in all of us and will return to the scene of burial or of the dwelling place of the deceased, there to avenge some offense. One can imagine the heightened sense of fear the Code Talkers felt as soldiers died around them; and these evil spirits brought another invisible threat.

This heightened sense of fright and confusion may be what prompted Cozy Stanley Brown to revert to an ancient Navajo ritual in the heat of battle. After killing a Japanese soldier, he actually scalped the enemy as he had been taught by a medicine man, Stewart Greyeyes.

As we follow the Code Talkers, island by island, we can truly appreciate their courageous contribution to our success in the South Pacific.

PAVUVU, NEW CALEDONIA, GOODENOUGH, NEW ZEALAND, AUSTRALIA

After spending time in the battle zone, the Code Talkers came to these islands for further training. They had learned many things under fire, and had to employ new ways of sending messages and new names for places, ships or weapons. Now they had an opportunity to learn from their problems in the field, to devise faster, more efficient operating procedures. Although it happened infrequently, when a code word had to be changed, the new word was passed to headquarters back in the States. Sergeant Johnston also was informed about what was happening at the front.

Revising the Code was hardly a challenge for the Code Talkers, but living on Pavuvu Island was. Here they confronted rats–big rats–and huge land crabs. The place was dirty and, to make matters worse, the Navajos were always asked to do the clean up. Being the most "seasoned among the group," William McCabe insisted that the sergeant help too. No doubt to Corporal McCabe's surprise and delight at being able to give an order to a superior, the sergeant complied and later made McCabe corporal of the guard.

On Pavuvu the Code Talkers along with Indians of other tribes danced the Yé'ii Bicheii, a ceremonial dance. Men, dressed as Yé'ii or spirit gods, dance close together in a line to a monotonous beat. It is one of the more public dances of the Navajo and can take several forms depending on the purpose. Following cultural lines, some of the Indians from Oklahoma, not Code Talkers, also did a dance. A Zuni Indian sang songs. On one side of the room was Hitler's picture, on the other side was Tojo's picture. As the dancing came to an end, one of the performers stabbed Hitler's picture while another stabbed Tojo's. These ceremonies were designed to protect them from the enemy on Okinawa, their next destination. The dances reflected the Code Talkers' need for security and protection in a strange and brutal environment.

In New Caledonia, there were about eight Code Talkers. Some took their paratrooper training with the 1st Marine Parachute Regiment there. Apparently jumps were never made in combat by the Code Talkers, and the paratroopers were disbanded in 1944.

On Christmas Day, 1943, William McCabe left Goodenough Island for the combat zone, and Frank Thompson left New Zealand for Guadalcanal.

After Camp Pendleton, California, the first stop for Jimmy King was Guadalcanal. It was also the first time under fire for William McCabe. McCabe took part in the first landings on this island but was sent again as a replacement because the Japanese had been deciphering a written code that they had found. The Navajo Code Talkers, working only by memory and with the ability to change code method as needed, was a definite advantage.

At first, the Code was not generally accepted in the field, and it was some time before McCabe was allowed to use it. Even though they were armed with a presidential order to report only to the Commanding General, the eight Code Talkers involved in the Guadalcanal operation were summarily put aside. Under fire for the first time, they were frightened and unsure of themselves. They found out very early that bullets went through the coconut trees behind which they were trying to hide.

At long last, or so it seemed to the Navajos, the General brought them to a colonel who, in turn, brought them to a lieutenant for duty. McCabe's words to the lieutenant must have been a bit startling:

National Archives

> They told us to report here and start talking. We're supposed to talk the enemy to death. We're not here to fight. We just came here to talk. That's what the message says.

Having no alternative, the lieutenant tried them out. There was much jamming and interference from the United States forces because they had never heard such talk and assumed it was the Japanese. Even the commanding general put them to a final test when he had them compete with a machine in sending a message. The Code Talker's message was received and confirmed in two and a half minutes while the machine took about four hours. McCabe then explained to the general, "We're just a walking coding machine . . . that's all. Whatever the other guy says it goes through his ears. It comes out uncoded." After that, it was not necessary to prove the Code Talkers' worth to anyone on Guadalcanal.

Sometimes the messages were given to Code Talkers by runners, or fuzzie-wuzzies. While these fuzzie-wuzzies outranked the Code Talkers, they soon realized their importance and would do anything asked of them. They would carry the Code Talker's gun, his ammunition, his canteen, even the soldier himself.

Finding a high place to dig their foxholes on the island, the Code Talkers watched with awe and fascination as the spectacular and fierce battle of the Coral Sea raged between the United States Navy and the Japanese fleet. It was "like the Fourth of July," said McCabe.[2] Frank Thompson was with the 1st Marine Division that took over the Matanika River and then continued on to the other end of Guadalcanal island. Finally, Guadalcanal was secured, due in no small part to the Code Talkers.

When R.O. Hawthorne was assigned there, the fighting was over. However, the men did not rest. They trained and retrained, having learned what it was like to send messages under fire from the enemy.

TARAWA

As the United States forces began their offensive, some of the smaller islands were secured quickly. It took only 72 hours to completely occupy Tarawa. Casualties remained high with over 1,000 men lost in that short period of time. Frank Thompson didn't have a chance to use the Code because the battle was over so quickly. However, he did have a close call when he and his partner, John Willie, Jr., were setting up their radio equipment. A small light was needed to see the radio numbers at night. After turning on the light as they worked, a bullet suddenly whizzed between their heads and hit the radio. After that, they quickly procured ponchos and used the light only under cover.

In 1944 Frank Thompson left Tarawa for Hawaii for rest and relaxation. He was preparing to return as a replacement when his ship blew up in the harbor. He was missing for three days. While he doesn't remember the details, he somehow managed to get to shore and was hospitalized in Honolulu. While still in bandages, he was put on another ship. This time he was headed for Saipan.

CAPE GLOUSTER

When Jimmy King landed on Cape Glouster in 1943, it was monsoon season. Heavy rains in the black of night and the orders of "no lights" and "no cigarettes" made survival a nightmare. In the dark night, feeling his way around and trying not to get lost, King was mistaken for a Japanese soldier. With a bayonet at his back, he ran into a foxhole where, by good fortune, he was identified as a Code Talker by a soldier he knew. With the battle continuing around him, King was found by a runner who told him his radio had been knocked out. He crawled inch by inch stringing new lines, all the while being shot at, soaking wet and in fear for his life. But, he knew the message must get through. And get through it did.

On Cape Glouster two Code Talkers were lost. Ralph Morgan was killed when a bomb that had not exploded split in two by a palm tree. Part of the bomb decapitated Morgan. Bennie Cleveland walked into a machine gun nest but was saved by a wounded Marine. It is ironic that Cleveland, after he returned to the States, is reported to have collapsed and died in a boxing match.

Tom White, because he looked Japanese, was able to clean out a pillbox all by himself. He stripped to the waist and just walked in. The Japanese thought he was one of them. He shot from the hip with a submachine gun and completely wiped out the enemy nest. He was able to do this with another pillbox, but was later killed on Peleliu. No citations were given for his heroism.

Paul Begay was another Navajo Code Talker who became a hero. Stripped of his uniform and looking like a Japanese soldier, Begay went through enemy lines and headed for the Division Command Post. He got the information that was needed, but had to run out again because his radio was not functioning.

On a few occasions, the Code Talkers were able to figure out the enemy's secret code words or gestures. Dennis Cattlechaser was one of them. Because he, too, looked like the enemy, he was able to invade the Japanese line. Then, by observing that they kicked each other two times as they crawled along in the dark rainy night, he realized that this was their way of identifying each other. Cattlechaser quickly kicked back two times and easily was able to crawl through the front line and back again to his own unit. Cape Glouster turned out to be a jumping off point for James Nahkai, Jr. and his partner, Lloyd Oliver. From here they went to Peleliu, from Peleliu to Okinawa, from Okinawa to Tientsin, China–all the while using the Code.

MARSHALL ISLANDS

In the Marshall Islands, Dan Akee saw his first dead Japanese. Because of the Navajo fear of the dead (that evil spirits are released and may inhabit one's own body) this was one of the most difficult obstacles he had to confront. In his twenty-five days there, Akee was forced to overcome his fear. It wasn't easy. In the midst of fierce fighting on these islands, there were dead all around him. Akee described his great concern about all the evil that was surrounding him:

> one of the most fearful things . . . to the Navajos was a
> dead body . . . And the shooting was going on . . . and I saw

some dead Japanese. . . . And I tried to glance at it, you know, but I just can't help it, you know. I just have to be among all those deads, you know, dead people. So that was one of the hardest things to get over. And finally I did.

For Dan Akee, overcoming his fear of the dead was surely as traumatic as the battle itself.

SAIPAN

Hilly and mountainous Saipan was the scene of another bloody and vicious battle in the South Pacific. Raphael Yazzie landed there after the island had been shelled by United States forces. He found everything in deplorable condition. The natives of the island had many chickens that were still flying around. Coconut trees were decimated. Dead Japanese were everywhere. There were several casualties among the landing forces, but Code Talkers Peter Sandoval, Jesse Smith, William Kien, Albert Smith, Danny Akee, Curtis Toledo, George Chavez, Carl Pinto, and Cecil Tsosie survived.

In the hills above Garapan, Frank Thompson and his partner had pulled back to rest. They were told the Army would now take over. Finally, the weary Code Talkers could get some rest. Suddenly came the last of the Japanese banzai attacks, so close by that Thompson lost his hearing for a week. In the darkness it was impossible to tell who was who. The Japanese had broken through the Army lines and taken possession of the Marine artillery. The Marines had removed all the firing pins so the Japanese couldn't use their ammunition. Consequently, they soon ran out of fire power but left their "calling cards" in the form of personnel booby traps. Books, pens, swords, pistols, anything that might be a souvenir was rigged. The demolition squad were heroes. Frank Thompson learned on Saipan that the four pronged item that he had picked up with curiosity on Tarawa was a personnel booby trap. It didn't explode and he threw it away, still not knowing what it was until later when he was shown a similar item on Saipan and warned about its deadly potential.

Sidney Bedoni remembers arriving on the island in time to hear the Japanese speaking in English: "American, you're going to die." "Come on out and fight, American." The enemy was able to hide in trees, dress in leaves for camouflage and imitate birds, all very effectively.

As the island was being secured, Wilfred Billey had his one and only opportunity to shoot his 45. A lone Japanese soldier kept walking in the water, ignoring all orders given in Japanese to surrender. Finally, the order was given to shoot. Everybody followed the order, but no one knows whose shot hit the fatal blow.

The food on Saipan, as well as the other islands, consisted of C-rations or K-rations until the island was secured. While these rations were probably designed to be nutritious, they left much to be desired in flavor. The staples of the Navajo Reservation, even today, are mutton stew and fry bread, much preferred to the White Man's rations, as Dan Akee points out:

> . . . life was different between an Indian and a white man, the way I find out over there, you know. And C-ration was not very good. We hardly have good, warm meal, you know, from landing till 2 or 3 weeks later, till we nearly secured the island is the only time we have a good meal. So it happened that we were on Saipan there, and Samuel Holiday made a sling shot. And there was lots of chickens that belonged to these natives who was living on the island there. So these white men, they don't know how to make a stew. So we kill one and got a, oh, kind of a big can there. Put some water in and start it boiling and cut and, of course, everybody was watching us, saying, "What are you doing, Chief?"
>
> "Well, we're gonna make a chicken stew." And we did, you know. We cook it and everyone wants a taste of warm soup there. And from there everybody ... wants to take part in killing the chickens around there. Even the colonel, he says, "Grab me one, Samuel." Well, he was a good

shot, you know. He slingshot and he kill chickens. Everybody was boiling chicken soup right around there all day, you know. Everybody liked it. Well, that's the time another K-ration came out, you know. Well, this had cookies in there that was so hard that sometimes you just got tired of eating. So this new ration came out with some bacon in. And I was sitting there and I wondered how can I make this cracker soft. So I was watching I was just warming some bacon, you know, in the morning. So I just tossed this hard cookie right into that pan there. And I thought about frying bread, you know. "Will you show me how to fry bread?" [asked] one of my buddies always with me, and his name was Robert Holmes. He was a white man. So I turned the thing over and then I took it up and it was really soft. And he started doing that too, afterward. And everybody say, "How did you make it soft?" "Oh, very simple." You don't know what fry bread means. And so I got the idea to soften these cookies. So we start doing that, you know, and everybody was doing that too.

Some of the Code Talkers arrived on Saipan after the fighting was over, but they weren't the only ones: the 4th Marine Division, the Navy, and the Air Force with B-29's had arrived earlier. Sidney Bedoni was there when the atomic bomb was dropped on Hiroshima. Bedoni, along with other Code Talkers, had been trained as a paratrooper, but none of them had ever jumped in the war. The landings were always from a Navy vessel. McCabe was also there when the war ended. He was told he would be going back to the States by air. After all he had been through, he didn't want to take a chance with an airplane, even a friendly one, and he resisted. He did, however, come back on a plane, with the hope that he would never have to fly again.

The story is told by General Greene (then a Colonel and Chief of Staff of the 2nd Division on Saipan) about General Watson ("Terrible Tommy Watson"). During the height of the battle one of the Code Talkers was on the line trying to get a message from the front lines. General Watson, impatient and no doubt irritable from the battle, kept repeating to Colonel Greene, "What's he saying? That Code Talker's talking with no translation. Go over–kick him–ask him what he's saying." The Code Talker, in exasperation, turned around and said, "He say, 'No.'"

TINIAN

In contrast to many of the Pacific islands, Tinian was flat, and therefore, most of the B-29 bombers were stationed there. The planes would depart, drop their bombs and return. Sometimes the coordination between the units was less than perfect, occasionally resulting in the front lines being shelled by their own men. On Tinian the code talking of the Navajos was a distinct advantage. The Japanese spoke excellent English and could easily send the wrong commands out onto the air waves. Because they were never able to decipher the Navajo Code, the Japanese were unable to sabotage our communications.

PELELIU ISLAND, *now known as* REPUBLIC OF PALAU

William McCabe carried the division flag when he went ashore at Peleliu in 1944. He had no chance to secure the flag because enemy resistance was very heavy for some ten days or more.

Because McCabe was so busy, Colonel Hennigan volunteered to plant the flag, but was killed in the process. As with the other islands, casualties were heavy there, too. There were shellings from Bloody Nose Ridge every night. Big guns hidden in caves in the mountains were secured with steel doors that opened when the guns were used. Twenty-six soldiers were bunched around the radio when it was hit. Only four got out alive. McCabe survived the attack because the other three survivors dug him out of the sand where the concussion of the attack had blown him. Several Code Talkers lost their lives. Tom White was killed by a Japanese colonel on a banzai charge. Harry Tsosie was killed by field artillery[3].

For Jimmy King the roughest battle was on Peleliu. He was called upon to be a stretcher bearer because casualties were so heavy. He also became a rifleman and a machine gunner serving wherever he was needed. Most of the time he was a Code Talker. As the senior Code Talker on the island, King had great compassion for his men. In his own words:

> Well, the one that had been burnt in my memory is that's where my men suffered the most. The longest hours without being relieved. Without water, without even food and medical attention, and there were so many of them that got hurt. And I couldn't send anybody out there. And I taste the blood and the sweat. I crawled. I leaped. I ran. I laid motionless–playing dead at times.

Code Talker Tom Singer was lost here. Singer seemed to have knowledge that he would not survive. He had given Jimmy King the pictures of his family. He asked King to contact them, not to tell them he had been wounded previously, but that he was all right.

Iwo Jima

Iwo Jima was an especially hard-fought battle. It took almost a month for the United States forces to secure this tiny island. Many Americans remember it because of the now-famous picture of the flag being raised as the forces captured Mt. Suribachi. The Code Talkers played a major role in taking Iwo Jima.

Paul Blatchford, stationed on the headquarters ship, noticed that the first two divisions attempting to land couldn't make it and had to regroup before reaching the beach. He also noted that the landing boat was heading straight in, rather than zigzagging. Blatchford suggested the zigzagging method to the colonel, who urged the third wave coxswain to pay attention to the "Chief." As a result, the third wave was the first wave to make a successful landing.

Under murderous fire, Blatchford and another Code Talker dug their foxhole and started sending messages. The Japanese started speaking in what sounded like the Navajo language and shelling a part of the island that they could see. Blatchford and his partner kept talking and sending the Code while the Japanese became more and more excited and continued to shell the wrong area. Not knowing what was happening, a Japanese-American soldier was called by the Code Talkers to listen to the exchange. He laughed at what he heard. "Just go ahead," he said to Blatchford. "They're excited. They think you're going crazy, too. They don't know who you guys are."

After stops at Tinian and Saipan, and after enduring a severe storm, another Code Talker also hit the beach at Iwo Jima. The enemy was everywhere. The order came to move up nonetheless. Carrying all of his equipment, all the time sending messages and saying his silent prayers, the man moved ahead. Suddenly, his radio no longer worked. There on the sandy beaches of Iwo Jima– under enemy artillery fire and with a panicky Anglo soldier beside him–he managed to get out his spare parts and fix the radio. Then he moved on.

One of the men had taught himself Japanese while on a ship going to the front. He learned quickly from a booklet given to him after his training. On Iwo at night he was able to let his fellow soldiers know where the enemy was by speaking out in Japanese. Sometimes they would answer or even send up a flare. The trick worked very well.

The Japanese had a few tricks of their own. At times, they would bury themselves in the sand, pretend they were dead and suddenly attack when a Marine passed by.

Some of the men do not talk much about their experiences on Iwo because they were so terrible, but one incident remains. One night a Code Talker and a "white guy" had made a foxhole and were taking seven-hour watches while the other slept. The enemy was so near "you could smell them." Unfortunately, the "white guy" fell asleep on his watch. The Code Talker awoke with a start to find the enemy about to enter the foxhole. He drew his knife ("I was good with a knife," he said), then cut the throat of the invader, severed his head and presented the head to his sleeping companion when he woke up. His white companion never slept on watch again!

Thomas H. Begay arrived on Iwo Jima on his 17th, "or maybe his 16th" birthday. He was assigned to the general at communication headquarters to replace another Navajo who had been hit. Later on the north side, he was in the front lines with the 24th Marines. Medicinal brandy was handed out to the men, and some who had never seen the ugliness of war drank to excess. Unfortunately, they then forgot all precautions and were killed by the enemy.

Paul Blatchford had not slept for four days when his group started up Mt. Suribachi. The machine gun fire was vicious. The many Joshua trees[4] on the island, with their roots protruding above the ground, made a perfect hiding place for the small Japanese soldier. Our men were being hit from every angle.

Suddenly, a United States flag appeared at the top of the hill. Then it disappeared, our soldiers still under fire. The fighting continued. Soon after, to everyone's joy, a second and bigger flag appeared. The Code Talker's message triumphantly spelled out: S-U-R-I-B-A-C-H-I. The now-famous picture, etched in our collective memory, was taken. Iwo Jima was in the hands of the United States forces.

Some of the Code Talkers who were on Iwo knew Ira Hayes, the Indian in the famous picture (even though he was not a Navajo). While alcohol apparently caused his death after he had returned to civilian life, his friends on Iwo knew him as a "nice, quiet boy who didn't drink."

Philip Johnston tells of sitting in Major Conner's offices listening to the epic of Iwo Jima:

The entire operation was directed in the Navajo Code, he [Conner] said. Our Corps Command Post was on a battleship from which orders went to three division command posts on the beachhead and on down to the lower echelon. I was signal officer of the Fifth Division. During the first forty-eight hours while we were landing and consolidating our shore positions, I had six Navajo radio nets operating around the clock. In that period alone, they sent and received more than eight hundred messages without an error.

OKINAWA

Okinawa was the last major operation of the Marine Corps. There were approximately forty to fifty Code Talkers there at one time; one was at headquarters and one or more at each of the battalions.

Out of all the 5th Marine regiment, Code Talker Alex Williams, Sr. was selected to go with the famous war correspondent Ernie Pyle. He was put in charge of the communications journal, sending and receiving messages, all in code. Ernie Pyle liked the Marines and made the unit famous as he interviewed the men. From there, he left to go to Okinawa and the small island of Ie Shima, where his jeep was hit by machine gun fire and he was killed.

JAPAN

Work was not over for the Code Talkers when the Japanese surrendered. Several were in the occupation forces in Japan.

Paul Blatchford and Rex Malone were assigned to the Army and Navy Intelligence when they arrived at Sasebo, Japan. Going ahead of the troops, they relayed messages to Navajo Code Talkers stationed in San Francisco, describing the devastation in Nagasaki from the second atomic bomb. They found temporary sheds built from the pine trees "just like the Navajos make." Inside were wounded Japanese civilians using newspapers to bandage their burns. Reports were also sent by Blatchford and Malone about conditions in the airplane factories that they visited.

Wilfred Billey found it hard to believe that one bomb could do so much damage. In all of his fighting he had never seen anything comparable. As he describes the devastation:

> . . . we camped in old naval, old military academy about three or four miles from Nagasaki. There practically all the windows had to be replaced . . . because how destructive it was. And we visited where they drop the bomb, and all the railroad rails were all twisted up and of

course, the buildings were just flat, burnt.

Thomas Begay was on his way to Japan by ship when the Japanese forces surrendered. When he landed with the occupation forces, he was no longer assigned as a Code Talker. Instead, he was made a trusted carrier for the cryptographic message center. He traveled all over Japan with messages in a courier pouch handcuffed to his wrist.

A few of the men did enter Hiroshima: "They said there used to be a big city there–nothing there, just flat."

CHINA

Some of the Code Talkers were sent to Northern China during the fighting between the Nationals and the Communist Chinese. The mission of the United States forces was to hold the railroad from the Communists. R. O. Hawthorne stayed for a year in the area, landing at Tsingtao and going from there to Tientsin and Peiping. James Nahkai, Jr. was around Tientsin still sending messages using the Code. However, messages were fewer and often papers were used which had to be hand carried for distribution. His unit did round up quite a few Japanese, however, and took them as prisoners.

The Pacific war ended with the formal surrender of Japan on September 2, 1945.

The Code Talkers had been an integral part of that war. The Code remained unbroken and was only declassified when sophisticated electronic methods replaced humans. Now it remained for the Code Talkers to be honorably discharged and to return to the life they had known. But could they? Would it be possible for them to resume life on the Reservation with all that they had seen and experienced?

One Code Talker was very concerned as he was about to be discharged. He repeatedly asked about his benefits as a veteran. He wanted to be sure he could attend school and learn a trade for, as he said, "I sure can't make a living on the Reservation just by talking."

Notes on Chapter V

Some of the direct quotes in this chapter are taken from the Doris Duke Collection, as noted in the Introduction of this book.

1. Langille, Vernon, "Indian War Call" (*The Leatherneck*, March 1948), p. 37.
2. While the late William McCabe remembered this as the Battle of the Coral Sea, he is probably referring to a later battle which he witnessed in July.
3. There is some uncertainty about where Harry Tsosie was killed. He may have been on Bouganville.
4. This is as the Code Talker remembers them. However, in all probability these were not true Joshua trees or Yuccas. There are a few trees that do produce roots or "knees" that do rise above ground or water level and can become quite massive. In the heat of battle the name "Joshua tree" may have seemed most accurate to the Code Talker.

Eight Code Talkers gather for a television show in 1976. Kneeling from left to right: Sidney Bedoni, Harold Foster, Paul Blatchford, Joe Kellwood. Standing from left to right: James Nahkai, Jr., Carl Gorman, Keith Little, Dean Wilson.

CHAPTER VI

Back Home:

Honors and Problems

MUCH HAS BEEN WRITTEN about the aftermath of World War II – its social, cultural and economic impact. From the individual tragedies of death and dismemberment to the family tragedies of broken homes, unfaithful spouses, financial disasters and psychological scars, the Allies and Axis nations both suffered a great deal from the war.

The Navajo veteran was subject to all of these repercussions plus an array of specific problems unique to his cultural background. The Navajo Community College[1] has documented that, proportionately, there were more Navajos fighting in World War II than there were other Americans. Consequently, the impact of what happened after World War II was magnified for the Navajo.

The Navajo veteran having been accepted, for the most part, into the Anglo war culture expected the same treatment when he returned to his homeland. The Code Talker, having worked with the sophisticated electronic equipment of the time, now was faced with a home that did not have electricity. World War II may have been a "coming out" of the Navajo Nation but much remained to be done before Anglos and Navajos would truly understand and accept each other's culture.

Well into the twentieth century, clans and the extended family were still important on the Reservation. It was this strong sense of family commitment that brought many men back after the war. Here they could relate to Anglos who were equally eager to get home to their families. The Navajo, however, was going home not only to the extended family but also to the world of the medicine man, a world of ceremonies, of holy mountains and of pastoral living that few Anglos would ever experience.

William McCabe wanted to go back to Ganado where he had been born. "I have some tree roots already dug for me and, boy, I'm gonna hang on to those tree roots," said McCabe.

Richard Kontz, the son of the late Code Talker Rex Kontz, told me of his father's experience as he reentered civilian life. He was nearing his home on the Reservation and, knowing that the Reservation was dry, he stopped at a nearby bar for a beer to celebrate his homecoming. The Anglo tavern keeper, not realizing and probably not caring about Kontz's brilliant war record, threw him out saying, "We don't serve Injuns here." This seemingly small incident had a great effect on his children as the elder Kontz told and retold his story.

The Navajos often met with such prejudice, especially off the Reservation. When this prejudice took the form of curiosity most of the Code Talkers were tolerant. Paul Blatchford relates:

> I went to Milwaukee and Detroit and I walked the streets there, and there was a group of us Navajos and we saw a bunch of white guys. I mean boys, they said, "Injuns, look at the Injuns!" Well, we didn't get mad. If they are happy to see Indians, well, so what?

Thomas Begay believes the "Navajos can get along with anybody, whether he's black, white, green, yellow; we're pretty adaptable." However, when the prejudice took forms other than simple curiosity, the Code Talkers were not so tolerant.

Prejudice had more modern, sophisticated forms, too. For many years, tourists had been coming to the Reservation to see such natural wonders as the Painted Desert and the Grand Canyon. Now there was a new flock of archaeologists who invaded Navajo territory, fascinated by the recent findings of the "ancient ones" in abandoned Chaco Canyon and of the still-inhabited Canyon de Chelly. Unlike early missionaries who often insisted that the Indian give up his language and his heritage in order to become civilized, Anglos now arrived who were curious about the Indian culture and wished to learn more. Thus, the Navajo Nation became a spotlight for Anglo researchers who were actually asking the Navajo Nation to stand still while they researched it. This was not the cultural exchange the Code Talkers had experienced during the war.

As with many soldiers after the war, some Navajos didn't want to return home. Not only did some Code Talkers not return home, but a few were never heard from again–even by their parents or other relatives. In addition to an assimilation with Anglos, several Code Talkers married women from other tribes further integrating the cultural and ethnic mix.

Jimmy King has tried unsuccessfully to get in touch with two Code Talkers who had sweethearts in Australia. He thinks they married and stayed there. He knows of several others who did not return, some even staying in Japan. Others who had no family on the Reservation would say to King, "I love that country, but I don't think I can ever go back." King says that the Navajos call such emotions the "unspoken feeling" and that only those who have gone through the hell of war can understand it.

Family ties brought some men back to the Reservation: lack of them kept others away. Some of those who felt no kinship to an extended family or who were orphans had no reason to return to the land of sheepherding and farming. Jobs were scarce. Opportunities were greater in thee Anglo world. After all, they had lived side by side with Anglos throughout the war. They now knew, or thought they knew, what the outside world was like.

One Code Talker already had a wife and three children when he enlisted. Despite having a family on the Reservation, he didn't come back immediately because his wife had been living with another man and had an out-of-wedlock child. Instead, he roamed around the country "here and there" until his wife discovered he had returned. Out of concern for his own children, he finally returned to his wife and the Reservation.

Some returning Code Talkers rejected the old traditions, the *Navajo Way*. No one person, even the Navajo, can know all the cultural implications of the various chants. The medicine man studies and learns these chants for many years and usually knows but one, or possibly two, healing ceremonies. There are many ritualistic items, such as the medicine bundle, the prayersticks, specific prayers, sandpaintings and plants with certain qualities. All these objects and many, many more are important, but the healing only takes place when they are used selectively and correctly by the medicine man in his rituals.[2]

Jimmy King feels a strong religious tie to his people. He believes that religion is now the only part left of the old *Navajo Way* and that it must not be taken away. His prayer and the prayer of other Navajos is "Dear Heavenly Father, what we have left we want to keep and hold–from now until the end of time." Despite his strong feelings that all else has been taken from the Navajos by the Caucasians, he bears no animosity toward the White Man. He feels they came here "with equal thought [and] an equal opportunity" and it was necessary for the Indian to surrender his material possessions, but not his ideas or his religion.

King feels that the religious ceremony performed for him before he left for the South Pacific sustained and upheld him during the war. His ceremony was based on a prayer meeting ritual held by the Plains Indians because as a child he was raised in the Plains Indian tradition. Now he presently takes part in all Navajo ceremonies, and feels that he knows the culture of both tribes. He speaks both languages fluently.

Even though Sidney Bedoni came from a traditional family, he did not have a ceremony when he went into the service. However, when he was on furlough, his family made a feather for him. The feather was kept in a safe place, and from time to time the family would take it out and pray to it that he would be all right. Sidney describes the Squaw Dance held for him when he returned:

> I took all my clothes off and then went into the hogan. Leave my clothes out there, my uniform . . . Get all washed up and everything. See, all that stuff that's on you, they think it's evil or something like that. They trying to chase them away . . . That all my mind won't be way overseas or anything like that. All my mind will come back to me when they have that Squaw Dance for me.

94

Bedoni still has the feather made for him but he forgets to carry it with him as he is supposed to do.

Paul Blatchford remembers having a ceremony on Catalina Island while he was in training. A sweathouse[3] was built which he says is probably still there if the authorities didn't find it. Chester Tso, who was learning to be a medicine man when he was inducted into the Marines, conducted the ceremony.

As a Baptist minister, R. O. Hawthorne believes that these ceremonies stay with the Navajo as a cultural experience rather than a religious belief. This may be the kind of evolution that took place among many of the Code Talkers. Some of those who had Enemy Way ceremonies performed for them when they returned did so at the request of parents and not because of their own strong religious beliefs. Belief in another religion (Christianity, for instance) can and does exist simultaneously with the Navajo cultural experience.

John Benally says that the religious aspects of the Enemy Way, one feature of which is now called a Squaw Dance, has become a less important part of the ceremony.

Originally the first night of the dance was preparation for the war party. A drum was made from certain raw materials. A dance to the beat of drumming simulates an actual battle. Contact with the enemy was made with a prayerstick (a clip with feathers and vegetation attached). After this contact the rest of the dance involved getting back to the original place, finally arriving home with guns heralding a successful mission. Now instead of an exclusively male dance, women are allowed to participate. Young unmarried women, in particular, are permitted to make a choice from among the young males; hence, the name Squaw Dance. The four days and four nights of the dance have now become a social gathering.

Before World War II most war ceremonials had died out. Certain rites were revived during the war, however, especially for those who had contact with non-Navajos either in the service or in war industries.

When Dan Akee returned from the war, he had terrible nightmares. He had gone deaf, and yet the doctor could find nothing wrong. Every time he closed his eyes the Japanese were coming for him. "I was laying in the hogan there, very sick," he says. Finally his father had a Gourd Dance performed for him.

> It was just unbelievable what happened to me. The first night I heard this drum, you know, and my ear popped out and I could hear again . . . And from there at this Gourd Dance I gain my . . . weight back and all this nightmare was not bad.

While the Anglo might say it is superstition, the Navajo believes that "like cures like" so evil may be necessary to have healing. Thomas Begay thinks that even though a ceremony might help him, in order to have that healing for himself, someone else may be hurt. He believes this because a Squaw Dance had been planned for him, and on the day the ceremony was to begin, his uncle was killed in a car accident. Begay says that had it not been for this ceremony, his uncle would be alive today. He has refused to participate in ceremonies since because he doesn't want to be responsible for hurting anyone else. Some of the Code Talkers did carry the "medicine pouches" from their ceremonies into war as talismans. Some believe that the ceremonies by the family back home saved their lives.

Alex Williams, Sr. had the traditional Navajo ceremony performed for him before going to war. It lasted three days. On the first night the medicine man began with prayers. The second day he received various talismans: dried yucca leaves, necklaces and belts in Navajo colors. The final all-night sing, conducted by the medicine man, involved parents, relatives and many other tribal members.

Mary Gorman informs me that

> "...some men had ceremonies, leaving or returning, that are of the Native American Church. Some had the protection ceremony, Where the Two Came to Their Father. This was also performed on return as a purification ceremony. The Enemy Way is performed to cleanse the mind and illness caused by the killing. It, as all ceremonies are, is reli-

gious, but Navajo religion deals primarily with the mind and healing, protection and the restoration to harmony. Many Navajos who profess to be Christian will come back to the *Navajo Way* when seriously ill, and the ceremonies are what brings the mind back to harmony and health. The Squaw Dance is the social part of the ceremony and has probably always been. Community support is part of the healing process whether the Enemy Way, the Yé'ii Bicheii, or the Fire Dance or any lesser performed ceremony when there are dances. I do not know of any other war ceremonies although there may have been. Where The Two Came To Their Father had probably not been performed between World War I and World War II." [4]

Today the Navajo Community College is trying to carry on these traditions. The medicine man still practices but often cooperates with the doctor. Dr. Taylor McKenzie, for many years the only Navajo physician on the Reservation, suggested the establishment of an American Indian School of Medicine. The school would train Navajo medical doctors who would be able to work with the medicine man. In this way native healing practices and modern medicine could solve some of the Navajo's health problems. Peter Iverson[5] reports: "Carl Gorman's efforts in the Navajo Healing Sciences Program promoted understanding of traditional Navajo healing and supported its practice. Gorman wrote a series of articles on Navajo health and healing and served as a liaison between traditional Navajo healers and Anglo physicians."

Upon returning to the Reservation, many of the Code Talkers wanted to make some changes to alleviate poverty and acquire more material possessions.

The launching of the Sputnik satellite by the Soviets on October 4, 1957, saw the Anglo world react with new emphasis on scientific education. Not understanding the educational efforts made by Navajo parents, grandparents and the extended family, Anglos saw the Indian falling further and further behind in educating their young. Many Code Talkers saw great promise for themselves, their families and the Navajo Nation in the educational opportunities offered to all returning veterans by the G.I. Bill.

Wilfred Billey, discharged in January 1946 did not have a high school degree. Starting in the summer of 1946, he finished high school and went on to three colleges–the University of New Mexico, New Mexico State and the University of Wyoming–emerging with a Master's Degree in Education.

The Reverend R. O. Hawthorne went back to school after returning from the Korean conflict and decided to become a Christian. He attended the Orthodox Baptist Institute at Ardmore, Oklahoma, the Clarksville Bible College in Tennessee and the Ohio Christian College. Then he served several Baptist churches off the Reservation before coming back "home."

Thomas Begay knew that if he wanted to remain on the Reservation, he would have to go to school and go to work.

"If I didn't," he says, "nobody's going to hand it to me. The same way with livestock. If you're lazy, sleep until eight o'clock or go to bed before . . . sundown, it's no use you going in the sheep business because you got to get up before sunrise . . . So it's in anything, you know: work, job."

Frank Thompson "fooled around" for about a year collecting monies owed him from his war service. After that, he realized he would have to get more schooling or find his first job. He used the first year of his G.I. Bill but let the other three run out when he found a good job as a carpenter. He regrets not having used all of his educational opportunities but has done well in running the tribal maintenance department.

As one of the first combat Marines to return from overseas, Sidney Bedoni became a local hero when he came back to his high school in Tuba City. The teachers and students alike learned a great deal from his interesting stories about the military experience.

Raphael Yazzie went to the Haskell Institute for vocational training. He felt that he did not have the background for college.

Peter MacDonald, an underage volunteer in the Marine Corps, came back from overseas to attend college. He became an engineer and worked for Hughes Aircraft before being called back to the Reservation by his friend, Raymond Nakai, then the newly elected chairman of the Navajo Nation.

Carl Gorman, one of the original Code Talkers and now a lecturer, philosopher, artist and teacher, holds, in addition to a certificate from Otis Art Institute, an honorary Doctorate of Humane Letters from the University of New Mexico. He has taught in two colleges and two universities.

Education, then, seemed to be one of the keys that could open the door to the white man's world for the Navajo. Education became both bilingual and bicultural. For those Navajos who wished to receive education beyond high school level, it meant leaving the Reservation. While this was important, it offered no exposure to the moral and cultural background of the Navajo. Consequently, in the early 1950s Raymond Nakai began to speak of a Navajo College.

Later in that decade, with the help of Arizona State University, plans were made for starting the Navajo Community College, an institution that is unique in several ways. It is an attempt to educate all Navajos so that they might relate not only to the Anglo but to the needs of their fellow Navajos. In addition, they might learn and be proud of their own heritage. The college also seeks to preserve the symbols, customs and language that are unique to the Navajo people. Courses are offered in such subjects as Navajo history, language, arts and culture among others. Many of the buildings are built in the shape of a traditional hogan. One of the main buildings has its entrance facing the East. Quite a few of the Code Talkers saw the need for this new institution and wholeheartedly supported its development. Even though there were rough days ahead, the Navajo Community College would remain and become a major force on the Reservation. After all, it was the first such institution of higher learning on any Indian reservation.

The College capitalized on the teaching talents of many Code Talkers, including Carl Gorman. Henry and Georgia Greenberg,[6] in their biography of Carl Gorman, tell of his many trips from Window Rock to Tsaille (60 miles away). Here, he lectured and instructed at the College in Navajo heritage and culture. The long drive over winding roads gave this artist and philosopher time to "reflect and commune with his thoughts."

Carl Gorman is an outstanding example of a Code Talker who made known the needs, wants, and beliefs of the Navajo people to other cultures not familiar with them.

Many of the other Code Talkers worked for the Bureau of Indian Affairs (BIA). Paul Blatchford came back to work first as a much-needed carpenter in Gallup, then became a skilled mechanic and worked in Phoenix for fourteen years. In 1959, he returned to Tuba City where his talents were more fully recognized and worked as a liaison interpreting tribal traditions for the BIA. He also became a member of the public school board and the Arizona State Education Advisory Board in Phoenix. As he says, "So that's my main purpose here is to tell 'em about Navajo. Some of their history, their way of life, what to expect when they get out there, how you encounter the Navajos and all that."

James Nahkai, Jr. became a force in the political life of the tribe after he returned from the war. For 23 years he was the Postmaster at Tohatchii, running a small grocery store in connection with the post office. In addition, he became a member of the Tribal Council and the New Mexico Human Rights Commission, Chairman of the Budget and Finance Committee and was elected to the Board of Directors of Navajo Forest Products.

Thomas H. Begay became head of Employment Assistance at Chinle. Begay is adept at translating all the various dialects of the Navajo language and used this ability many times as an interpreter for Anglo Senators and other outsiders. As head of Employment Assistance, Begay helped young people find employment. This group established educational grants for Navajos and helped them find jobs, on and off the Reservation. As Begay says, "It is necessary to go where the opportunities are," and he is there to help with the adjustment to the outside world.

Of course we explain this to the people . . . a city, they have bars, maybe one block has thirty of them, all kinds of bad things, bad streets, slums. We talk about this . . . that they are going to have to pay rent, they can't live off these, as you do here. The laws are changed and different. You get picked up for drink or something, 90 days or 100 dollar fine. Here is ten bucks. No relative is going to bail you out. So this is the difference.

Many words have been written and spoken about the BIA, and the Code Talkers have not been reticent in their opinions. The BIA, run by the federal government, was traditionally operated by the Anglos.

After World War II, many Navajos became involved, not just as workers but as policymakers. Many Code Talkers had a say in management. Others agreed with the perception depicted in Carl Gorman's painting, *The Rope*. The painting portrays a wild horse tethered to a rope (the BIA) straining to get away. According to former Marine Sergeant James Dawkins, a friend of Mr. Gorman, the gathering storm clouds in the background are representative of the Navajo people. (A softer version of the meaning of this painting is contained in Henry and Georgia Greenberg's biography of Carl Gorman.[7] The Greenbergs write: "He [Carl Gorman] said that it came out of his feelings for what men did to animals and for what other men had once done to his Navajo people.")

The opinion of Paul Blatchford is far more conciliatory, regarding the BIA. When asked whether the tribe should take over the BIA, his reply was, "We hate to see that. This will go back before he white man even came to this country . . . we'll be fighting each other." He also quotes Annie Wauneka, a distinguished Navajo Council-woman who said she went to a place where chickens were green, pink, red, blue . . .

And she noticed then how they were getting along together even though the colors were varied . . . but they all worked together. She said somebody asked that question, "what do you think about the Navajo taking over?" That's what she brought out, and she says, "We don't want that all white, all black. We don't want that. We want it just like that . . . different colors on our Reservation." I'm thinking just the way she think . . . that we don't want the Indians to take over . . . not to take the whole thing over. We still need everybody. We need Chicanos . . . We need Anglos . . . different races to be in with us. Ask just the Navajos to kick out the BIA–NO. We want the BIA in there too.

Annie Wauneka was still strong in her opinions when interviewed in 1988. Her recent editorial (March 1, 1990) from the Scripps Howard News Service began with the headline: "Scrap the Bureau of Indian Affairs." The editorial went on to explain how "a new Senate committee report details the agency's record of waste, corruption and mismanagement." Obviously, this is an area that needs further investigation by the Navajos and other Indian tribes.

Paul Blatchford thinks that some of the functions of the BIA should be taken over by the Navajos, particularly where Navajo culture is involved. He cites the boarding school dormitories: "Anglos are in charge, but they don't actually understand the culture." He has asked parents about using Navajo aides. The response has been enthusiastic. "They (the students) don't get lonesome . . . They don't run away . . . (the aides) are older people and they tell them stories at night . . . and they feel as they are at home." Here, Blatchford contends, is where the Navajo should take over. "But for the school, I don't think so. I think we should have it all mixed . . . teaching . . . we should have all different nationalities. That's the way to learn."

In matters of law, the increasing involvement with outsiders made the Navajos realize that they needed to establish a judicial system of their own. Although there were Navajo attorneys, state courts would soon take over unless a Navajo Nation court system was established. Instead of Navajos deciding their own fate, Anglos would again be deciding it for them. In 1960, several Navajo judges were appointed, among them Code Talker William Dean Wilson. Since the men had little legal expertise, the task was a difficult one. Training seminars, usually under the aegis of university law schools, were held, but the problem was to balance Navajo beliefs and justice with federal and state laws. It became necessary for the judges to interpret the law to their fellow Navajos.

Even off the Reservation, the Code Talkers became a force in making known the needs, wants and beliefs of the Navajo people. Carl Gorman, along with Peter MacDonald, lived in Los Angeles and often attended an interdenominational Indian mission church. Here they could talk with other Navajos in their own language, could reminisce, tell stories and celebrate their common culture.

After the war, conditions on the Reservation were poor. Winters were difficult. And jobs were scarce. More and more Navajos began going to Los Angeles seeking employment and a better life. Gorman realized that a special sanctuary was needed where these Navajos could be with their own. When Myron and Virginia Denetdale proposed The Navajo Club of Los Angeles, Gorman, MacDonald and others accepted the proposal wholeheartedly. The Club became a major help to Navajos unfamiliar with Anglo ways. These Navajo "relocatees" were often hungry, in need of counseling or other assistance. They were too proud to accept public welfare. The Navajo Club, with Gorman as its chairman, provided help wherever possible. Not only did the Navajo Club help its own, but its members tried to provide to others an understanding of Navajo culture through talks, dances and ceremonies.

Honors for the courageous Code Talkers have been slow in coming. Immediately after the war, the Code was classified as top secret. It was thought that it might be needed again. However, by the late 1960s, electronic equipment had advanced enough so the Navajo Code could be declassified. The final Code used in World War II is found in Appendix C.

One of the great disappointments for Philip Johnston was the sudden elimination of the PFC rating he had recommended for, and which was promised to, all those graduating from the Code Talkers' classes. While some of the men came from boot camp with PFC rating, others did not and Johnston had to tell about sixty men that the promised rating was denied. He believed they took it well with no ill feeling. Johnston may have misinterpreted the silence with which the Navajos accepted the announcement. One of the Code Talkers says that, while he was not in the group denied the rating, he heard talk about it when he was on liberty. Further he says:

> Most of the boys probably think the same way I do. They promise you something . . . then they don't come out with it. See, in the white culture, verbal's not good enough. It's to be in black and white. When they just tell you that it couldn't be done, it seems as you're getting cheated out of something that was given to you at first.

Frank Thompson thinks that one reason so few Code Talkers were decorated was because they were always in the thick of the battle. Nobody had time to recommend anyone or had much chance to see another's heroics. He thinks that about 50% of the Code Talkers deserved a medal and that several should have receive a Congressional Medal of Honor.

Finally, in June 1969 a medallion was struck by the Franklin Mint.

The medallion front and back pictured here, was presented to the Code Talkers on June 18, 1969, in a ceremony in Chicago.

A search was undertaken to find as many 4th Division Code Talkers as possible. In addition, one representative of the other five divisions were invited. They were brought to Chicago to receive their bronze medallion in a long-overdue ceremony designed to recognize their contribution in the war. On the left side of the medallion is the painting, *Ira Hayes, His Dream–His Reality* by Joe Ruiz Grandee. It depicts Ira Hayes, a Pima Indian riding his Indian pony. On the right side and in the background of the medallion is depicted the famous picture of the raising of the flag on Mt. Suribachi on Iwo Jima. It is the picture snapped by Associated Press photographer Joe Rosenthal and printed in all U.S. newspapers at the time. The medallion is hung on rawhide that is strung with red, white, and blue Indian beads. The banquet and the presentation of the medallion were a fitting tribute to a group of men who were relatively unknown but who played a major role in the United States victory in the South Pacific.

At the 1971 reunion of the Code Talkers, the decision was made to form a Code Talkers' Association. This association is fraternal and educational. In 1975 a telethon raised money for the men to participate in the Tournament of Roses Parade in Pasadena, California, and in 1976 money was raised through another telethon in Phoenix to send the group to Philadelphia and Washington, D.C. where they march-ed in the United States Bi-centennial Parade. And march they did with great and justifiable pride.

On the State Capitol grounds in Phoenix there is a stone monument listing the Navajo Code Talkers among other Arizona war heroes. Tom McCarthy of Tesuque, New Mexico, made for Onewest Media of Santa Fe a 28-minute movie of the Code Talkers in which many of them, including deposed chairman Peter MacDonald, talk of their experiences.

Would the Code Talkers be able to send messages today as they did over forty years ago? There is little doubt that they could. Martin Link, then curator of the Navajo Tribal Museum, speaking about the First Annual Reunion of the Code Talkers held in 1971 said:

> But then we had a couple of radio units that the Marine
> Corps furnished. We had one up on what is now C-ration
> Hill and the other one over on the ridge on the other side of

the fairgrounds here. The men had a very enjoyable time relaying messages back and forth, and especially I think an official message that Jimmy King (composer of the Marine Corps Hymn in 1943) wanted to relay in that he wished the Navajo people success and health and happiness in all times, considering even this time of drought that we're going through now. And then, "God Bless America" at the end of the message, all relayed in Code.

This statue, honoring the Code Talkers and sculpted by Douglas Hyde, stands in the Phoenix Plaza. As the plaque says, the flute "is a communications tool used to signal the end of confrontation and the coming of peace."

In 1989, I had the privilege of attending the ceremonies honoring the Code Talkers given by the Heard Museum. In the Phoenix Central Plaza a statue and plaque were dedicated in their honor. The sculpture stands ten feet high, depicting a Navajo boy with a flute in his hand.

The next day, in front of many onlookers, the Heard Museum presented the Code Talkers with further honors and asked them to demonstrate Code Talking as they used it during the war. Except that they were not under fire, the men worked in pairs just as they had on the battlefield, relaying messages quickly and accurately.

The demonstration was a huge success–the men were still able

The author, Two Code Talkers and a Navajo woman (wife of Code Talker on left) at the Heard Museum ceremonies in 1989. Notice the beautifully worked Navajo jewelry.

The demonstration was a huge success–the men were still able to use the Code, translate it into English and tell the gathered audience what had been said. A truly remarkable feat for men mostly in their late sixties and seventies (some of whom were plagued with illness) and who had not used the Code in over forty-five years. After all that time, these remarkable men still retained their Code!

Recognition is coming at last to this valiant group of Navajos. As it comes, so too will an understanding of their culture within the Anglo culture, of their Nation within a Nation.

At the 31st annual Indian Fair held at the Heard Museum, Vincent Craig, son of Code Talker Bob Craig, sang his original ballad called "Code Talker." As reprinted from the *Phoenix Gazette* of March 2, 1989, the words that follow are a fitting tribute to those men who meant so much to their country:

He's the son of the Four Directions,
And a child of the Blessing Way,
raised in the loving arms
of his mother
Wisdom comes to him
through the legends of long ago,
told by a man who loved
the wandering eyes of a little child.

My daddy was a Code Talker Man
with Uncle Sam
He spoke on the whistling wind
during the time of man.

He packed his bags and got on the train,
headed for L.A.,
off to fight a war
that he really couldn't understand,
goodbye to the four sacred mountains
of his youth.
But he shall return,
for the medicine bag is strong.

A dark foreboding piece of land
somewhere in the South Pacific,
a place called Iwo Jima,
destiny had brought him here.
Many of you will die–
Oh, that's what they told him then.
Perhaps he thought of home
and his people the Navajo.
Remember me, my four sacred mountains.
Help me to understand the pain
that he suffered there
during the time of man's inhumanity.

Notes On Chapter VI

Some of the direct quotes in this chapter are taken from the
Doris Duke Collection as noted in the Introduction of this book.

1. The name of Navajo Community College has recently been changed to Diné College.
2. For the reader who wishes more precise and detailed information on the various ceremonies, a number of books have been written on the subject, in particular,

> Reichard, Gladys A.: *Navaho Religion* (University of Arizona Press: 1983);
> Zolbrod, Paul G.: *Diné bahane* (University of New Mexico: 1984);
> Sandner, Donald: *Navaho Symbols of Healing* (Harcourt Brace Jovanovich: 1979).

3. A sweathouse is a hogan in which the men gather after shedding their clothes. Heat from fire and hot stones makes the men sweat. The men will stay in this atmosphere for many hours while prayers and ceremonies are performed by the medicine man.
4. Mary Gorman is the widow of Carl Gorman, Code Talker, philosopher, artist, teacher and statesman of the Navajo Nation.
5. Iverson, Peter: *The Navajo Nation* (Westport, Connecticut and London: Greenwood Press, 1981), p. 159.
6. Greenberg, Henry and Georgia: *Carl Gorman's World* (Albuquerque: University of New Mexico Press, 1984), pp. 164, 165.
7. Ibid.

CHAPTER VII

Epilogue:
Personal Reflections

As I DROVE FROM the Colorado border to Window Rock, it was a glorious October day in Navajo country. The rains mixed with heavy snow–so typical of autumn in Colorado–had not yet arrived. The paved roads of the main highways were easily passable. The sun in the cloudless blue sky shone through the Window Rock in the Navajo Nation's capital and spread warmth through the area. Nearby, Shiprock appeared to sail through the plains to rescue The People (Diné) just as it had in prehistoric times. We saw herds of sheep coming from even higher country to their winter corrals. Shepherds on horses were coaxing and leading the recalcitrant ones. I wondered: With all this beauty and tranquillity, was life as easy and as calm for The People as it appeared on the surface?

My first stop in Window Rock was a visit to Council Chambers and the area where so recently there were reporters from all over the world attempting to follow the story of Peter Mac-Donald's troubles with the law.

When I arrived, the government buildings gave no hint of the 1990 turmoil. Peterson Zah was now President of the Navajo Nation. The Council was not in session but would be in another week or so. I was looking for the headquarters of the Code Talkers' Association. Later in the week I discovered that it had been moved to the Chamber of Commerce building in Gallup, New Mexico. My search led me to the public library: a well-stocked, crowded basement room in the complex of government buildings. The bookmobile was out and seemingly doing a brisk business in the surrounding area on the Reservation.

My search also led me to Kee Long, Media Specialist II of the Public Relations Office. From him I learned about the strict new rules for the making of motion pictures, television commercials and broadcasts on the Reservation. Not only must these productions be accurate but also in an attempt to combat high unemployment, the producers must employ as many Navajos as possible.

One of the highlights of my 1991 trip to Window Rock was a visit with Tom Arviso, Jr., editor of *The Navajo Times*. I have subscribed to this leading Navajo newspaper since 1979 and have seen it go from a small four-page weekly, to a stint as a daily, to going out of business and now to an impressive, full-color 16-page weekly format. I was eager to meet the editor who obviously had a great deal to do with the newspaper's present success.

Tom Arviso, Jr. is a personable, easy-to-know, single (divorced) parent of three. He was raised in the traditional *Navajo Way* and hopes to raise his children with some of the same precepts. We talked about education on the Reservation. The boarding schools still exist. Tom's mother teaches at one. Very small children, taken from the protective atmosphere of the extended Navajo family, are frightened and difficult to teach.

On a recent trip to visit his mother, Tom found a young boy alone and crying in the hallway. Thinking he was in trouble with the school authorities, Tom stopped to see if he could help. To his surprise he discovered other children were making fun of the boy because he had no laces for his shoes. Tom kept his mother waiting while he bought a pair of shoelaces. Perhaps it was not only poverty that led to the lack of shoelaces, but also the disassociation of the child from a caring, loving extended family.

Navajo children attending public schools must travel long distances by bus, usually leaving before dawn and arriving home after dark. While all children and teachers confront this problem in vast sparsely settled areas, it is particularly difficult for Navajo children because these Anglo towns and communities are so different from life on the Reservation.

The Navajo Community College currently has several branches. Its main campus is still in an unpopulated area, or as Tom says "in the boondocks." He suggests that the main campus be moved to Window Rock where he feels the college would be more effective in educating the youth of the Reservation. Conversely, there are those students who can travel the distance to a branch but cannot get to Window Rock. I met one young woman living in Cortez, Colorado (just off the Reservation) who is finding her course in the Shiprock branch enjoyable and most challenging.

Most men and women who wish to pursue a four-year college degree and/or graduate school do have to leave the Reservation. At the most vulnerable age (just as the Code Talkers did in an earlier generation) young Navajo men and women must now face the conflict of cultures as *The Navajo Times* so colorfully remarked "of coping with parallel realities." As the Code Talkers did, with the strong family background and strength of character, many young Navajos also will and do adjust. Just recently several Navajo students spent six weeks at a private high school in Connecticut. The cultural exchange was most successful for both Navajos and Anglos.

Unemployment on the Reservation is extremely high. Tom estimates it runs about 40%. Unfortunately, red tape makes it almost impossible to start a business even by Navajos. An entrepreneur thinks everything is settled, then finds more paperwork is necessary to get started. One must often go from bureau to bureau as part of a time-consuming, discouraging process.

Several large Anglo companies have attempted to set up branches on the Reservation. A few have actually been in operation. I found it difficult to get managers of these companies to talk about the problems. Suffice to say, many have discontinued operations on the Reservation. In a 1989 visit, I observed a thriving agricultural business (raising onions and potatoes) operated by the Navajo Nation with Navajo workers. This may be a forerunner of future activity.

Just recently, construction on a natural gas pipe-line across the Reservation had to be halted because of a dispute between the company's union and the prospective Navajo employees. The Navajos are not union members. Work on the Reservation is supposed to be given to qualified Navajos. For a while there was a standoff with Navajos on one side of the pipeline site and union members on the other. Bloodshed was avoided by the presence of Navajo and Arizona state police. The company had not been aware of the hiring regulation. Now negotiations are taking place and work on the pipeline will continue, hopefully, with Navajo workmen.

There have also been some takeover attempts by outsiders to acquire businesses on the Reservation. As Tom says, the *Navajo Way* is not to do evil to others. He was taught that such tactics would always come full circle and would hurt the instigator. He has found this to be true in all cases with which he is familiar.

There seems to be a growing discontent with the Bureau of Indian Affairs among the Navajo. Tom Arviso, Jr. feels that while other tribes may still need the help of the BIA, the Navajo Nation is now large enough and intelligent enough to handle the work of the BIA on its own. There is merit in his assessment of the Navajo Nation and its people. The Code Talkers' Association also notes that the Navajo Nation never gets the actual amount assigned by the federal government contracts. However, unless the BIA is discontinued gradually, there would be a major period of adjustment without Federal assistance.

Health on the Reservation seems to have improved. There are many more Navajos practicing medicine on the Reservation and attending medical schools. Just recently the first female Navajo doctor set up her practice. Following trends in the Anglo world, several diseases have been eradicated. Tuberculosis is no longer the threat to life on the Reservation that it once was. Although there are still many problems, access to facilities at city hospitals has improved.

For young Navajos no longer in school and unwilling to accept the farmer's life, the side effects of high unemployment hit hard. Even in this relatively rural area, a few gangs have been formed and held responsible for several highly publicized killings. The formation of satanic cults, an even more alarming development, has been associated with a number of hangings. These trends will bear watching.

On the positive side, many young Navajos I met are inspiring to observe as they take up employment on the Reservation. Life at the Navajo Nation Inn was pleasant indeed. Navajo employees of the Inn (which is run by the Navajo Nation) were efficient, friendly and very willing to help. In the West World Clothing Store on the Reservation, I met Grayson Claw whose Uncle Thomas Claw was a Code Talker now living in Parker, Arizona. According to Grayson, during World War II the United States maintained a large prison camp in Yuma. After the war the area was reclaimed by the Indians. Grayson's father, who was in the service but not as a Code Talker, and his uncle took land there and became farmers. Thomas Claw still lives and farms there and Grayson has many interesting telephone conversations with him. Grayson's father, on the other hand, could not stand the noise and heat in Yuma so he sold his land and returned to the Reservation. There he could enjoy peace and tranquillity and raise his family in the *Navajo Way*.

At the suggestion of Tom Arviso, Jr., I met with one of the sportswriters for *The Navajo Times* (all correspondents for the paper are part-time and are scattered throughout the Reservation). He is also a full-time teacher of video/communications and an athletic coach at Fort Wingate High School. He and his brothers are well educated; his degree is from Arizona State, one brother is a graduate of U.C.L.A., and the other is a Ph.D. This son of a Code Talker works long hours at two jobs, is divorced, but is planning to remarry soon. He has no children of his own but will take on his future wife's children when he marries. He is justifiably proud of his brothers and especially of his father. His father overcame many hardships on his way to becoming a Code Talker. He was sent to boarding school in Winslow for an education. The trip took four days by wagon where he slept in the open at night. As with many Code Talkers, the culture shock of entering the Anglo world of war was severe, but he was able to survive. Now he is retired but still very active. After rising at 5:00 a.m., he runs four miles every morning.

Senator Barry Goldwater believed that because the Navajos are not used to living in typical towns or cities, they will always find it difficult living in the Anglo world. He contends that they are really

Togetherness. Navajos and Anglos enjoy a dinner of beef stew made by the Anglo hostess and fry bread made by the Navajo guest. Author is pictured at hostess' right and next to the Navajo couple's daughter.

nomads and want to be left to themselves. While this may have been true in the past, I question whether this is true today. Throughout my last eleven years of interviews and of just "getting acquainted," I have made many friends and found a genuine desire among the Navajo to know my world. This has been my goal: to know and respect the Navajo world. They do not wish to abandon their own culture. Nor do I wish to abandon mine. We wish only to respect and live together harmoniously and with mutual understanding.

There is evidence that, after many long years, Anglos and Navajos are beginning to adjust culturally to each other. Neither wants to surrender to the other's ways. The precise Navajo language should survive; some teachers do know both English and Navajo. Certainly the Code Talkers have been instrumental in helping to preserve the language. Even if it's "trading post Navajo, Anglos can learn the basics.

To be open to the learning process is important. An Anglo geologist who is a member of the Governor's Council of the Crow Canyon Archaeological Center, worked as a young man in the oil and mining fields near and on the Navajo Reservation. Soon after he arrived in one field, he was assigned a Navajo college freshman who said she wanted to study geology. He later learned that she wanted to understand her people and her history better. His first thought was that the girl could not possibly understand complicated measuring tables. So he assigned her only minor office tasks to keep her busy. To his great surprise he found her very quick. She absorbed information well and was able to do some very involved procedures. The company also had hired a young Navajo draftsman. He, too, was an excellent worker, but he didn't like living off the Reservation. He was homesick for his culture and for his people. After two years he returned to the Reservation.

In its educational program for students, Crow Canyon Archaeological Center in Cortez, Colorado tries to enhance the cultural understanding between the Native Americans and Anglos. In setting up a program for Chinle (a Reservation area) students, Megg Heath of Crow Canyon found parents were very concerned about their children handling original artifacts found in Navajo holy places. Evil spirits could be released. Sensitive to the parents' concerns, Crow Canyon made reproductions of all the artifacts their children would handle. This program was so successful that in March 1992 it was expanded to include other areas, such as Shiprock. Now the program includes a medicine man who explains the original meanings and some of the uses of these artifacts. Plans are also being made for Crow Canyon personnel to go to Chinle to experience firsthand another culture. Jerry Vincent, Director of Crow Canyon, says there were over 200 students, mostly Navajo, enrolled in 1990, and 300 signed up for 1991. Alvin Smith, the first Navajo student, picked up amazing skills and shared them with others, bringing a sense of continuity to the Navajo people.

Perhaps the best summation would be the answer Tommy Arviso, Jr. gave to one of my questions as we were getting acquainted. I asked him what he thought of the currently popular movie, *Dances With Wolves*–a movie purported to have an Indian point of view. With a smile he immediately replied, "It was good entertainment," but he continued that while it was somewhat overdone, the best scene was the little Indian child who was scared of the buffalo and who cries after the killings. This, he said, showed the Indian as a human being. The Indian is just as apprehensive and just as frightened as other humans in the world. The brave, stoic Indian is a false picture. The world needs to know that Navajos are the same in their humanity as are the English, Spaniards, Chinese, Japanese or Germans. We may have different beliefs about the supernatural, different forms of worship, different ways of raising children, different methods of providing for the family unit, but that is all they are: different.

War does not solve the internal problems of the combatants, but it does bring many changes. This was especially true for the Navajo Nation after World War II. Changes came quickly and far too fast for many traditional Navajos. The Code Talkers who had already faced a "foreign" world and learned to adjust were able to bridge some of the gap. Many became the "elite" on the Reservation. The Anglo, unfortunately, often did not and sometimes still does not, comprehend that a change in his attitude towards the Native American is necessary.

Without a doubt the Code Talkers who came back to the Reservation after the war played a major role in helping Navajos understand the "outside" world. As teachers, guidance counselors and parents they told their children what to expect when they left the Reservation. The young people were told they would be enticed by the bars. There would be no one to tell them when to stop drinking. There would be prejudice. Jobs would be difficult to find and keep. They would have to find a place to live and pay rent. There would be temptations. The extended family would no longer be there to help. All of this the Code Talkers tried to impart to their young.

Even Peter MacDonald,[1] who seems to have thought that the use of power to increase his personal wealth would also increase

Window Rock

the power of his people, extols the virtues of the *Navajo Way* in his articles and speeches.

For me, after more than eleven years of association with the Navajos and the Code Talkers, the answer to the question "Did the Code Talkers make a difference?" is clear. They did indeed help in securing the Pacific Islands during World War II. Since then, the Code Talkers and their Nation have helped us to understand that humans can respect cultural differences and can learn to live in harmony.

In their art, their music, their poetry and their prose, the Navajos have proclaimed to the world the *Navajo Way*. In the tradition of these stories and myths, the Code Talkers used their code only by memory. Now the written language is the vehicle by which stories can be read in either Navajo or English.

I am impressed by the Navajo's spiritual beliefs. The moral precepts of the *Navajo Way* lie deep within the soul of the Navajo. Humankind, so goes one belief, is blessed with two bodies: one the Outside Body, the other the Spiritual Body.

J. Black

The Deer Hunter's Prayer

*O Great Spirit, let your winds be gentle and
your skies be heavy;
Let there be a fresh blanket of snow on the ground
To track the antlered one as did my forefathers.
Grant that I find him with antlers like tree branches,
wide and mighty,
And grant that my hands be steady and
my aim be true.
But most of all, O great Spirit,
Grant that my children and their children's children
Have the wisdom to preserve your work in forests,
fields and streams
So that they too can one day hunt the antlered one
In the footsteps of their forefathers.*

LEE KING, 1990

Therefore, the Indian can look at pain or hunger, realize it affects only the Outside Body and retreat to the Spiritual Body, thus looking at the pain or hunger from the outside. To an Anglo, this seems impossible. The Navajo knows it is possible. He becomes a part of all the earth. Mother Earth will nourish his outside body just as she does the trees, the birds, the insects, and the animals. Humankind cannot know poverty as long as the soul is singing. This spiritual life is movingly shared in song and in poetry. Vincent Craig's tribute to his Code Talker father, Bob Craig, which appears at the end of Chapter VI (page 108) is but one example. Lee King's poem and its artistic rendering by J. Black are on page 120. The world will lose much if it allows the simple truths of the Navajo beliefs to die. Although the way is still far from clear, the Winds of Freedom are in motion for all of us.

On March 10, 1994 a flag of the Commonwealth of the Northern Mariana Islands was presented to the Code Talkers Association in appreciation for the Code Talkers help in the liberation of those islands. Representative Juan N. Babauta in presenting the flag indicated that instead of

> "hailing their individual effort in liberating the Northern Marianas and their sacrifice that contributed to America's victory in the Pacific, some of the Navajo Code Talkers focused their concerns on the basic needs of those people whose lives had been affected by the tragedy of war. They asked whether the children today have schools to go to, is there a store available where people can get their groceries, and are people's homes that were destroyed during the war rebuilt? Those who developed a bond with some of the Chamorro and Carolinian children they rescued during the war wondered what became of them. Others were curious to find out if some of their island friends were still alive."

The Code Talkers were invited to the Marianas in 1995 to help celebrate the Fiftieth Anniversary of the landing on those islands, and a number of the Code Talkers did attend.

War, as Representative Babauta said, exacts a heavy price on the soul of humankind, and I echo to the Code Talkers his words:

> I humbly stand here to say that you and your deeds have not been forgotten."

My talk in 1993 with Albert Smith, past president of the Code Talkers Association, that we now wish to emphasize peace rather than war accomplishments, makes me want to end this section of the book as I began it, with the "Dedication to the Navajo Nation":

> *Your cultural heritage–*
> *Your spiritual orientation–*
> *Your willingness to forgive–*
> *Your love of family–*
> *Your belief in the Web of Life–*
> *The "Navajo Way" gives hope to a world in need.*

Millennium 2000:
What Does the Future Hold?

As we enter a new century, it has not been necessary to change the story of the Code Talkers. As the years go by they stand even taller in the minds and hearts of the American people.

Most of this book has been concerned with the experiences of the Code Talkers themselves. As an Anglo looking at this story, I have added my own comments; however, it occurs to me that mine should not be the only comments about the Code Talkers' work. To that end – and I hasten to add this is not a "scientific" survey – I have talked with several who had knowledge of or worked with the Code Talkers in the field.

Because of the nature of the Code Talkers' service, such as using the Navajo language and the necessity of the secrecy of the code, the Navajos kept much to themselves. Remember also these were very young men just off the Reservation, often for the first time, having to cope with a totally unfamiliar environment and culture. One Anglo, after living for some time in a remote area of the Reservation, understands the awe and wonder of lights and sound of another culture as she, too, reentered her Anglo culture. She found the sight of a neon sign in the distance a cause of both excitement and fearful anticipation, much like the young Navajo about to be a Code Talker must have felt. It is then very natural that the intermingling with other soldiers would be brief and only in connection with the work of sending and receiving messages.

Robert Hodgson, now a retired geologist with a Ph.D from Yale University, entered the First Marine Division as an 18-year old Anglo. In his words he "survived basic training", a comment with which many Code Talkers would agree. That same basic training, however, gave all mixtures of cultures a unity of experience that was distinctive to the Marines, and would give the Code

Talkers, the Anglos, and those of Spanish or African descent, a certain sense of belonging to an elite group of soldiers.

Mr. Hodgson did well on the exams for radio school and was trained to repair and service radio equipment. He, as were the Code Talkers, was trained at Camp Pendleton. As a radio man (Corporal), he, too, carried 30 pounds of radio equipment on his back, which, along with his other equipment, meant about 70 pounds that he carried into the field. His equipment needed three men to set up and run.

It was on Peleliu that Hodgson first came in contact with the Code Talkers. With the use of earphones and code machines, Hodgson's equipment could receive and send about 30 miles. Even though codes were changed regularly, there were problems particularly as to the speed of transmission and the ability of the enemy to decipher. Finally came the decision to go to voice communication. It was then that the Code Talkers were sent in. Because the enemy was so close, U.S. planes needed to drop their bombs very near our own troops. Here the Code Talkers were invaluable. They could relay very quickly the exact location of the enemy and also the exact location of our own troops. The enemy was completely baffled, according to Hodgson. The Code Talkers rendered a service to their country the depths of which will never be completely known.

After Hodgson was discharged, he reentered Yale and subsequently went back to the Navajo Reservation to do research for his geology dissertation. He and his wife, whose story is told above, found the Navajos to be both friendly and helpful with his research. This, combined with a great sense of humor on the Navajos' part, made the Hodgson's stay on the Reservation memorable.

While I was giving a talk about the Code Talkers to a historical society, one man – during the question/comment period said that he, too, had been in the Pacific during World War II. While he did not know any Code Talkers personally, he and his fellow soldiers always knew the Code Talkers had been there paving the way for the U.S. troops to take over.

Robert M. Neiman was a young Marine in the Pacific during World War II. He, too, commented on the bulkiness of the equipment and the fact that it took "runners" to string lines. By today's standards such machines seem to have been only the beginnings of what was to come in voice communications. Neiman was "glad we had them [the Code Talkers] because of the trouble they caused the enemy. They drove the enemy "crazy" in his words.

Robert Wallack, Private First Class, an 18-year old was in the thick of battle with the 29th Division of the Marine Corps in the Pacific. He served on Saipan, the Mariana Islands, Okinawa, and Ryuraya Islands. His was an interesting story of the use of "war dogs" (Doberman). He said the Japanese rubbed some kind of perfume on their bodies. Wallack presumed the Japanese believed this to have been some sort of protection for the soldier. Because the enemy troops moved mostly at night, they could not be seen; but, according to Wallack, the war dogs could sense the perfume odor and would tug on their tethers to alert the trainer as to where the enemy was hiding. Then would come in the "unsung heroes", Wallack stated. The Code Talkers would alert headquarters of exact locations, and thus the enemy was eliminated with less danger to the U. S. troops.

We are told that no survey is ever 100% accurate. Perhaps my small – and unscientific – poll of non-Native Americans has set a record. Even among those I talked with only casually, there was no dissension as to the admirable way the Code Talkers performed their service under the most trying and hazardous conditions.

World War II was an exception to many of the wars this country has entered since 1945. Everyone – from "Rosie, the Riveter" to the "Powder Puff" young women who flew the planes from factory to the Air Corps, from G. I. Joe to the most decorated General, from the WAVES and the WACS to the Navy , Marines, Army, and Coast Guard from the home front to the front lines, from corpsman to doctors– EVERYONE knows what and who he/she was fighting and why it was necessary. Therefore, all were heroes and heroines, and as I say a sincere thank-you and well-done to all of the Code Talkers, I want to also include those unsung heroes at home and abroad who brought the Winds of Freedom to all of us during World War II.

At Last! The Recognition

The Rotunda of the Capitol in Washington, D.C. was the site of an impressive ceremony to properly honor the Navajo Code Talkers and their contribution of a code that was never broken during World War II. The Code originally developed from the Navajo language will be found in this book in the Appendices.

Four of the original five Code Talkers were received by President George W. Bush in front of an invited audience on July 27, 2001. President Bush praised the heroes and awarded Congressional Gold Medals to the original Code Talkers present at the ceremony and posthumously to relatives of the remaining 24 who are deceased. These original Code Talkers were the developers of the Code.

Approximately 300-400 Navajos served as code talkers in the Pacific during World War II. Members of this group were honored with the Silver Congressional Medal on November 24, 2001.

In an article published in the *Chicago Tribune* of July 27, 2001 one of the Code Talkers, R.O. Hawthorne, who enlisted in 1943, said he was honored to have served his country by using his traditional language. "We count that as a privilege," he said. "We appreciate the recognition in this ceremony, but our real reward was the privilege to serve."

Headlines of this event were published throughout the United States. A listing of some of these articles are listed in the Notes at the end of this chapter[2].

Notes on Chapter VII

1. I cannot leave this discussion of the Code Talkers' influence after the war without paying special attention to Code Talker Peter MacDonald. As of this writing, he is under indictment, suspended from his elected office as Chairman (title has since been changed to President) of the Navajo Nation. Prior to his suspension, he had become the most powerful Navajo both within and outside of the tribe. MacDonald has made no secret of his goals for his people: complete control by the Navajos of their land, their resources, their labor and their laws. By his fourth inaugural address he had become completely committed to the *Navajo Way*:

> The wealth of our people IS our people. I am not just talking about individual Navajos. I am talking about how we can help each other: that is the *Navajo Way*.
> The most efficient economic system ever created is the family. The Navajo family, the extended Navajo family, the clans have strength greater than the nuclear family.

Unfortunately, the charge of misuse of funds has plagued Mac-Donald since he first returned to the Reservation in 1965 and later as head the Office of Economic Opportunity. Despite such rumors, he was elected for an unprecedented fourth term as Chairman.

Then rumors became charges. On October 18, 1990, with reporters gathered from all over the world, a six-member jury in Tribal Court found Peter MacDonald guilty on 41 of the 42 counts, for taking bribes and violating tribal ethics laws. His son, Rocky, was found guilty on 23 counts leveled against him. Peter Mac-Donald was sentenced to seven years and his son to two years. They are scheduled to go on trial in Federal Court on charges of bribery and conspiracy involving a tribal loan to Navajo Technologies, Inc.

Another federal trial is investigating the death of two Mac-Donald supporters in a July 1989 riot in Window Rock. This book will have gone to print before either of these cases is decided and probably before the MacDonald begin serving any sentences.

In 1990 MacDonald faced three tribal court trials. He was convicted twice and acquitted once. (*The Navajo Times*, January 18, 2001, page 1).

In 1991 MacDonald faced two federal trials. He was convicted and sentenced to 14 years in prison. He would have been scheduled for release in October 2005. On January 20, 2001 President Bill Clinton, as one of his last acts as President, commuted Peter MacDonald's sentence and that same day he was released from federal prison in Fort Worth, Texas. If he follows certain conditions put upon his release, he should remain a free man.

Although MacDonald now has serious health problems, he was a powerful man, both in the Navajo Nation and in the United States. He led the Navajo Nation for four terms as Chairman and President. At that time he was a great influence among his people. Polls show the people approve his release , and there are those who think he never should have been convicted. Now comes the "job of healing", as *The Navajo Times* calls the future. He has both opponents and supporters. MacDonald himself has apologized, "his heart is contrite for all the problems in his fourth term in office."

(For excellent summaries of MacDonald's convictions, both pro and con, and his return to the Reservation, see *The Navajo Times* issues of January 18 and 25, 2001.)

2. List of newspaper articles about the honors of the Navajo Code Talkers on July 27, 2001:

"Navajo Code Heroes of WWII Saluted on Capitol Hill", *Chicago Tribune*, Chicago, IL, July 27, 2001.

"Bush Lauds Indian WWII Heroes", *New Haven Register*, New Haven, CT, Associated Press, July 27, 2001

"Navajo Code Talkers to be Honored for WWII Role",
The Arizona Republic, Betty Reid, July 25, 2001.

"Code Talkers to Receive Congressional Medals',
Daily Courier, Prescott, AZ, Mary Perea, Associated Press,
July 25, 2001.

"W Hails Navajos of WWII",
New York Daily News, New York, NY, Associated Press,
July 27, 2001.

"Navajo Code Talker Enjoys Recognition",
The Spectrum, St. George, UT, Foster King, Associated Press,
July 27, 2001.

"Code Talkers To Get Congressional Medals",
The Spectrum, St. George, UT, Mary Perea, Assocated Press,
July 25, 2001.

"Bush Gives Congressional Gold Medals to the Original
Navajo Code Talkers",
Robert Gehrke, Associated Press.

"Navajo Code Talkers Honored",
Hartford Courant, Hartford, CT, Angela Turner, Assocated
Press, November 25, 2001.

"Day of Honor" (One of Top 10 Stories of 2001),
Navajo Times, Window Rock, AZ, January 3, 2002.

APPENDICES

APPENDIX A

*Philip Johnston's Proposal for Establishment of
The Code Talkers as Presented to
the Commanding General of the Amphibious Corps
Pacific Fleet, Camp Elliott, San Diego.*

1. GENERAL

The American Indian comprises a distinct racial subdivision, presumed by anthropologists to have migrated from Asia by way of the "land-bridge" at Bering Strait. Dates of these migrations have not been fixed, but recent excavations have disclosed human remains in association with those of the now extinct giant sloth–an indication that earlier migrations occurred more than 20,000 years ago.

Present Indian population of the United States is 361,816 comprising 180 tribes. These are divided into distinct linguistic stocks, each of whose languages has apparently evolved from a common source. The total number of tribes in the United States, Canada, and British Columbia is 230, which represents 56 linguistic stocks. The language of a tribe belonging to one linguistic stock is completely alien to that of another stock; and in most cases variations of the tongues within a linguistic stock may be so great as to be mutually unintelligible.

All Indian languages are classed as "unwritten" because no alphabets or other symbols of purely native origin are in existence. In a few cases, these aboriginal tongues have been reduced to writing by American scholars, who have developed alphabets adapted to the expression of the difficult consonants involved. A notable instance in point is the Navajo Dictionary compiled by the Franciscan Fathers of Saint Michaels, Arizona, who have also translated portions of the Bible, and written other texts in the Navajo tongue for the use of their students. Recently, the United States Bureau of Indian Affairs has inaugurated a program of writing Navajo texts for study in reservation schools. However, a fluency in reading Navajo can be acquired only by individuals who are first highly educated in English, and who, in turn, have made a profound study of Navajo, both in its spoken and written form. An illiterate Navajo is, of course, entirely unable to read his own language.

Because of the fact that a complete understanding of words and terms comprising the various Indian languages could be had only by those whose ears had been highly trained in them, these dialects would be ideally suited to communication in various branches of our armed forces. Messages sent and received between two individuals of the same tribe could not, under any circumstances, be interpreted by the enemy; conversations by telephone or short-wave radio could be carried on without possibility of disclosure to hostile forces.

2. Tribes Available for Recruitment

A logical approach to the problem of selection of suitable personnel for an Indian Signal Corps would be to consider the largest tribes in the United States. Reference to accompanying maps will show locations of each of the following:

Tribe	Population
Navajo	49,338
Sioux (in South Dakota)	20,670
Chippewa	7,443
Pima-Papago	11,915

The Pima and Papago tribes are so closely allied in language as to be mutually intelligible. Percentage of literacy among the foregoing tribes would be in direct proportion to the length of time each has been in contact with educational facilities. The Chippewa would no doubt have the highest percentage, with the Sioux second, the Pima-Papago third, and the Navajo fourth. It should be noted, however, that a prerequisite to effective service in transmitting code messages is an excellent command of both the native tongue and of the English. In some cases, individuals of a tribe that has had long contact with white residents may have largely forgotten his native tongue.

Since only a minute percentage of the foregoing tribes are college graduates, it is unlikely that 250 members of each, between the ages 21–30, would be available for recruitment. However, a fair number have attended government and public schools, and completed twelve grades, equivalent to high school. Without doubt a large majority of these would have sufficient command of both their native tongues and of English to qualify for service in the signal corps. It is also probable some individuals with even less schooling, by reason of constant use of the English language, might be qualified for signal corps service. This matter could readily be ascertained by giving each applicant an examination to show his fluency in both tongues.

3. RECRUITMENT OF NAVAJO INDIANS

This tribe is selected as an example of a possible plan for recruitment because of the writer's intimate knowledge of its reservation, the people, and their language. Most of the factors discussed would apply to the other three tribes in varying degrees.

With an area of 25,000 square miles, and an approximate population of 50,000, the Navajo reservation is one of the most sparsely populated sections of the United States. It is traversed by unimproved roads and trails; and many of its outlying portions are accessible only on horseback. Culturally and linguistically, the Navajo has been autonomous, and apart from surrounding white population. But in recent years, an increasing number of Navajo children have attended schools established by the government on this reservation, where they have received grammar school instruction; and a large percentage of these students have graduated from other schools of higher grades located at points remote from the reservation, where the curricula include native arts and crafts, as well as various trades and occupations taught in accredited schools throughout the United States.

Because the manner of life on the Navajo reservation provides small opportunity for educated Indians to set up a standard of living compatible with their training, a large portion of them have sought employment in government agencies and institutions, and in towns near the reservation. Therefore, an effective program to contact suitable personnel for recruitment would require publicity designed to reach every Navajo whose age and education qualifies him for service. The most important feature of such a program would be a bulletin prepared to set forth the following:

a) that the Navajos are in a unique position to render service in the defense of the United States—a service which will be of inestimable value.

(b) that such a service would involve the transmission of messages in their own tongue, which is not understood by any other people in the world.

(c) that meritorious service in such a capacity may result in advancement in the service.

(d) that applications for enlistment are received at designated localities.

The best location for a central recruiting station would be at the Central Navajo Agency, Window Rock, Arizona, or Gallup, New Mexico. Secondary stations for contact of local applicants should be located at several points throughout the reservation, preferably at Tuba City, Arizona, Chin Lee, Arizona, and Shiprock, New Mexico. Special efforts should also be made to contact Navajos through government school superintendents at Leupp, Fort Defiance, Kayenta, and Keams Canyon, Arizona and Crownpoint, New Mexico.

A considerable number of eligible applicants will also be found among the following categories:

(a) Navajos attending non-reservation government schools, such as those located at Phoenix, Arizona, and Albuquerque, New Mexico.

(b) educated Navajos employed at the foregoing schools and in various capacities by the government.

(c) educated Navajos who are employed off the reservation, principally in the cities of Flagstaff, Winslow, Gallup, and Albuquerque.

(d) Navajos who have already enlisted, or have been inducted into the armed forces, who might be transferred to the Marine Corps for special training in signal work.

4. INDIAN AFFAIRS OFFICIALS

Direct contact with the Navajo Reservation should be made through Mr. E. R. Fryer, Superintendent, Central Navajo Agency, Window Rock, Arizona. Contacts with proper authorities among the other tribes listed can be made through the Honorable John Collier, Commissioner of Indian Affairs, Washington, DC.

Original: Navajo Tribal Museum, Window Rock, Arizona

APPENDIX B

WORDS AND MUSIC
TO
"ALL IS BEAUTIFUL"

Naestsan Biyin
Song of Healing
(Hozhonji Song

Very quietly
and not too fast
m.m. ♩ = 132

Hi ne ya

Dal- tso ho-zho-re, ...
All is beau-ti-ful, . . . beau - ti - ful,

Dal- tso ho-zho-Ka',
All is beau-ti-ful,

Dal- tso ho-zho-Ka', hi-ye . . . .
All is beau-ti-ful, in-deed, . . .

Dal- tso ho-zho-re.
All is beau-ti-ful

Ko la ra ne

137

138

Aarstran Beym

8 Refrain.

Pelch Ka' alt-sin sel-la   ho-ush-te he ye

Meet-ing, join-ing one an-o-ther, help-mates ev-er, they,

Dal- tso ho-zho-Ka',

All   is   beau-ti-ful,

Dal- tso ho-zho-Ka', he-ye

All   is   beau-ti-ful, in-deed,

Dal- tso ho-zho-ne

All   is   beau-ti-ful

Ko la ra ne

Ka' Do-Ko-o-sled-i-ye, ye, Ka De-pe-ri-tso-ye,

Now Do-Ko-o-sled-i-ye, Kye, and De-pe-ri-tso-ye,

Ka'-la Tsha -al-yelah i ye, Ha yal-Ka-tli ye,

And the night of dark-ness,   and the dawn of light,

139

Aastran Beyn

Ka' Hast ye- yal- ti- ye- ye, Ka' Hast ye- ho- ga- ni- ye,
Now Hast ye- yal- ti- ye- ye, And Hast ye- ho- ga- ni- ye,

Ka' na- tan- alch Ka' i- ye- ye, Ka' na- tan- alch tso- i- ye,
And the corn, white corn, And the corn, yel- low corn,

Tra- de- tin- i- ye, An- alch- ta- ni- ye,
And the corn- pol- len, And the Re- pen- er,

Ka' sa- a na- ra- i, Ka' bi- ke ho- zho- ni- ye,
Life that nev- er- pas- seth, Hap- pi- ness of all things,

Dal- tso ho- zho- ni, ...
All is beau- ti- ful, ... beau- ti- ful,

Dal- tso ho- zho- Ka',
All is beau- ti- ful,

Dal- tso ho- zho- Ka', hi- ye . . .
All is beau- ti- ful, in- deed, . . .

140

The author is indebted to Dover Publications for granting permission to re-print "All Is Beautiful" from The Indian Book © by Natalie Curtis, Editor and Recorder, published by Dover Publications, New York, 1968.

The above picture is a copy of the original cover of Navajo Dictionary (The Navajo Code) used by the Code Talkers during World War II. This later edition was provided by the United States Marine Corps Historical Center, Washington, DC, after the Code had been declassified.

APPENDIX C

The Navajo Code

Appendix C contains "Navajo Dictionary,"
Official Document for the Code
as used by the Navajo Marines
in World War II,
Declassified DOD DIR 5200.9.

NAVAJO DICTIONARY

ALPHABET

A.	(Wol-la-chcc)	Ant	G.	(Ah-tad)	Girl
A.	(Be-la-sana)	Apple	G.	(Klizzie)	Goat
A.	(Tse nill)	Axe	G.	(Jcha)	Gum
B.	(Na-hash-chid)	Badger	H.	(Tse-gah)	Hair
B.	(Shush)	Bear	H.	(Cha)	Hat
B.	(Toish-jeh)	Barrel	H.	(Lin)	Horse
C.	(Moasi)	Cat	I.	(Tkin)	Ice
C.	(Tla-gin)	Coal	I.	(Yeh-hes)	Itch
C.	(Ba-goshi)	Cow	I.	(A-chi)	Intestine
D.	(Be)	Deer	J.	(Tkele-cho-gi)	Jackass
D.	(Chindi)	Devil	J.	(Ah-ya-tsinne)	Jaw
D.	(Lha-cha-eh)	Dog	J.	(Yil-do-i)	Jerk
E.	(Ah-jah)	Ear	K.	(Jad-ho-loni)	Kettle
E.	(Dzeh)	Elk			
E.	(Ah-nah)	Eye			
F.	(Chuo)	Fir			
F.	(Tsa-e-donin-ee)	Fly			
F.	(Ma-e)	Fox			

WORD		NAVAJO			LITERAL TRANSLATION
K.	(Klizzie-yazzie)	Kid	R.	(Gah)	Rabbit
			R.	(Dah-nes-tsa)	Ram
L.	(Dibeh-yazzie)	Lamb	R.	(Ah-losz)	Rice
L.	(Ah-jad)	Leg			
L.	(Nash-doie-tso)	Lion			
			S.	(Dibeh)	Sheep
M.	(Tsin-tliti)	Match	S.	(Klesh)	Snake
M.	(Be-tas-tni)	Mirror			
M.	(Na-as-tso-si)	Mouse	T.	(D-ah)	Tea
			T.	(A-woh)	Tooth
N.	(Tsah)	Needle	T.	(Than-zie)	Turkey
N.	(A-chin)	Nose			
			U.	(Shi-da)	Uncle
O.	(A-kha)	Oil	U.	(No-da-ih)	Ute
O.	(Tlo-chin)	Onion			
O.	(Ne-ahs-jah)	Owl	V.	(A-keh-di-glini)	Victor
			W.	(Gloe-ih)	Weasel
P.	(Cla-gi-aih)	Pant	X.	(Al-na-as-dzoh)	Cross
P.	(Bi-so-dih)	Pig	Y.	(Tsah-as-zih)	Yucca
P.	(Ne-zhoni)	Pretty	Z.	(Besh-do-tliz)	Zinc
Q.	(Ca-yeilth)	Quiver			

A.	Able	H.	How	O.	Oboe	U.	Uncle
B.	Baker	I.	Item	P.	Peter	V.	Victor
C.	Charlie	J.	Jig	Q.	Queen	W.	William
D.	Dog	K.	King	R.	Roger	X.	X-ray
E.	Easy	L.	Love	S.	Sugar	Y.	Yoke
F.	Fox	M.	Mike	T.	Tare	Z.	Zebra
G.	George	N.	Nan				

WORD	NAVAJO	LITERAL TRANSLATION

NAMES OF VARIOUS ORGANIZATION

Corps	*Din-neh-ih*	Clan
Division	*Ashih-hi*	Salt
Regiment	*Tabaha*	Edge Water
Battalion	*Tacheene*	Red Soil
Company	*Nakia*	Mexican
Platoon	*Has-clish-nih*	Mud
Section	*Yo-ih*	Beads
Squad	*Debeh-li-zini*	Black Sheep

OFFICERS

Commanding General	*Bih-keh-he (G)*	War Chief
Major General	*So-na-kih*	Two Star
Brigadier General	*So-a-la-ih*	One Star
Colonel	*Atsah-besh-le-gai*	Silver Eagle
Lieutenant Colonel	*Che-chil-be-tah-besh-legai*	Silver Oak Leaf
Major	*Che-chil-be-tah-ola*	Gold Oak Leaf
Captain	*Besh-legai-na-kih*	Two Silver Bars
Lieutenant	*Besh-legai-a-lah-ih*	One Silver Bar
Commanding Officer	*Hash-kay-gi-na-tah*	War Chief
Executive Officer	*Bih-da-hol-nehi*	Those in Charge

NAMES OF COUNTRIES

Africa	*Zhin-ni*	Blackies
Alaska	*Beh-hga*	With-winter
America	*Ne-he-mah*	Our Mother
Australia	*Cha-yes-desi*	Rolled Hat
Britain	*Toh-ta*	Between Waters
China	*Ceh-yehs-besi*	Braided Hair
France	*Da-gha-hi*	Beard
Germany	*Besh-be-cha-he*	Iron Hat
Iceland	*Tkin-ke-yah*	Ice Land
India	*Ah-le-gai*	White Clothes
Italy	*Doh-ha-chi-yali-tchi*	Stutter
Japan	*Beh-na-ali-tsosie*	Slant Eye
Philippine	*Ke-yah-da-na-lhe*	Floating Island
Russia	*Sila-gol-che-ih*	Red Army
South America	*Sha-de-ah-ne-hi-mah*	South Our Mother
Spain	*Deba-de-nih*	Sheep Pain

WORD	NAVAJO	LITERAL TRANSLATION

NAME OF AIRPLANES

Planes	*Wo-tah-de-he-ih*	Air Force
Dive Bomber	*Gini*	Chicken Hawk
Torpedo Plane	*Tas-chizzie*	Swallow
Observation Plane	*Ne-as-jah*	Owl
Fighter Plane	*Da-he-tih-hi*	Humming Bird
Bomber Plane	*Jay-sho*	Buzzard
Patrol Plane	*Ga-gih*	Crow
Transport	*Atsah*	Eagle

NAME OF SHIPS

Ships	*Toh-dineh-ih*	Sea Force
Battle Ship	*Lo-tso*	Whale
Aircraft	*Tsidi-ne-ye-hi*	Bird Carrier
Submarine	*Besh-lo*	Iron Fish
Mine Sweeper	*Cha*	Beaver
Destroyer	*Ca-lo*	Shark
Transport	*Dineh-nay-ye-hi*	Man Carrier
Cruiser	*Lo-tso-yazzie*	Small Whale
Mosquito Boat	*Tse-e*	Mosquito

NAME OF MONTHS

January	*Atsah-be-yaz*	Small Eagle
February	*Woz-cheind*	Squeaky Voice
March	*Tah-chill*	Small Plant
April	*Tah-tso*	Big Plant
May	*Tah-tsosie*	Small Planting
June	*Be-ne-eh-eh-jah-tso*	Big Planting
July	*Be-ne-ta-tsosie*	Small Harvest
August	*Be-neen-ta-tso*	Big Harvest
September	*Ghaw-jih*	Half
October	*Nil-chi-tsosie*	Small Wind
November	*Nil-chi-tso*	Big Wind
December	*Yas-nil-tes*	Crusted Snow

VOCABULARY

WORD	NAVAJO	LITERAL TRANSLATION
Abandon	*Ye-tsan*	Run Away From
About	*Wola-chi-a-he-gahn*	Ant Fight
Abreast	*Wol-la-chee-be-yied*	Ant Breast
Accomplish	*Ul-so*	All Done
According	*Be-ka-ho*	According to
Acknowledge	*Hanot-dzied*	Acknowledge
Action	*Ah-ha-tinh*	Place of Action
Activity	*Ah-ha-tinh (Y)*	Action Ending in Y
Adequate	*Beh-gha*	Enough or Sufficient
Addition	*Ih-he-de-ndel*	Addition
Address	*Yi-chin-ha-tse*	Address
Adjacent	*Be-gahi*	Near or Close By
Adjust	*Has-tai-nel-kad*	Adjust
Advance	*Nas-sey*	Ahead
Advise	*Na-netin*	Advise
Aerial	*Be-zonz*	Stinger
Affirmative	*Lanh*	Affirmative
After	*Bi-kha-di (A)*	After
Against	*Be-na-ghish*	Against
Aid	*Eda-ele-tsood*	Aid
Air	*Nilchi*	Air
Airdrome	*Nilchi-beghan*	Airdrome
Alert	*Ha-ih-des-ee*	Alert
All	*Ta-a-tah (A)*	All
Allies	*Nih-hi-cho*	Allies
Along	*Wolachee-snez*	Long Ant
Also	*Eh-do*	Also
Alternate	*Na-kee-go-ne-nan-dey-he*	2nd Position
Ambush	*Khac-da*	Ambush
Ammunition	*Beh-eli-doh-be-cah-ali-tas-ai*	All Sort of Ammunition
Amphibious	*Chal*	Frog
And	*Do*	And
Angle	*Dee-cahn*	Slanting
Annex	*Ih-nay-tani*	Addition
Announce	*Beh-ha-o-dze*	Announce
Anti	*Wol-la-chee-tsin*	Ant Ice
Anticipate	*Ni-jol-li*	Anticipate
Any	*Tah-ha-dah*	Any
Appear	*Ye-ka-ha-ya*	Appear

WORD	NAVAJO	LITERAL TRANSLATION
Approach	*Bi-chi-ol-dah*	Approach
Approximate	*To-kus-dan*	Approximate
Are	*Cah-tso*	Big Rabbit
Area	*Haz-a-gih*	Area
Armor	*Besh-ye-ha-da-di-teh*	Iron Protector
Army	*Lei-cha-ih-yil-knee-ih*	Army
Arrive	*Il-day*	Arrive
Artillery	*Be-al-doh-tso-lani*	Many Big Guns
As	*Ahce*	As
Assault	*Altseh-e-jah-he*	First Striker
Assemble	*De-ji-kash*	Bunch Together
Assign	*Bah-deh-tahn*	Assign
At	*Ah-di*	At
Attack	*Al-tah-je-jay*	Attack
Attempt	*Bo-o-ne-tah (A)*	Try
Attention	*Giha*	Attention
Authenticator	*Hani-ba-ah-ho-zini*	Know About
Authorize	*Be-bo-ho-snee*	Authorize
Available	*Ta-shoz-teh-ih*	Available
Baggage	*Klailh (B)*	Baggage
Banzai	*Ne-tah*	Fool Them
Barge	*Besh-na-elt*	Barge
Barrage	*Besh-ba-wa-chind*	Barrage
Barrier	*Bih-chan-ni-ah*	In The Way
Base	*Bih-tsee-dih*	Base
Battery	*Bih-be-al-doh-tka-ih*	Three Guns
Battle	*Da-ah-hi-dzi-tsio*	Battle
Bay	*Toh-ah-hi-ghinh*	Bay
Bazooka	*Ah-zhol*	Bazooka
Be	*Tses-nah*	Bee
Beach	*Tah-bahn (B)*	Beach
Been	*Tses-nah-nes-chee*	Bee Nut
Before	*Bih-tse-dih*	Before
Begin	*Ha-hol-ziz*	Commence From
Belong	*Tses-nah-snez*	Long Bee
Between	*Bi-tah-ki*	Between
Beyond	*Bilh-la Di*	Down Below
Bivouac	*Ehl-nas-teh*	Brush Shelter
Bomb	*A-ye-shi*	Eggs
Booby Trap	*Dineh-ba-whoa-blehi*	Booby Trap

| --- | --- | --- |
Borne	*Ye-chie-tsah*	Born Elk
Boundary	*Ka-yah-bi-na-has-dzoh*	Boundary
Bull Dozer	*Dola-alth-whosh*	Bull Sleep
Bunker	*Tsas-ka*	Sandy Hollow (bed-like)
But	*Neh-dih*	But
By	*Be-gha*	By
Cable	*Besh-lkoh*	Wire Rope
Caliber	*Nahl-kihd (C)*	Move Around
Camp	*To-altseh-hogan*	Temporary Place
Camouflage	*Di-nes-ih*	Hid
Can	*Yah-di-zini*	Can
Cannoneer	*Be-al-doh-ts-dey-dil-don-igi*	Big Gun Operator
Capacity	*Be-nel-ah*	Capacity
Capture	*Yis-nah*	Capture
Carry	*Yo-lailh*	Carry
Case	*Bit-sah*	Case
Casualty	*Bih-din-ne-dey*	Put Out of Action
Cause	*Bi-nih-nani*	Cause
Cave	*Tsa-ond*	Rock Cave
Ceiling	*Da-tel-jay*	Seal
Cemetery	*Jish-ch*	Among Devils
Center	*Ulh-ne-ih*	Center
Change	*Thla-go-a-nat-zah*	Change
Channel	*Ha-talhi-yazzie*	Small Singer
Charge	*Ah-tah-gi-jah*	Charge
Chemical	*Ta-nee*	Alkali
Circle	*Nas-pas*	Circle
Circuit	*Ah-heh-ha-dailh*	Circuit
Class	*Alth-ah-a-teh*	Class
Clear	*Yo-ah-hol-zhod*	Clear
Cliff	*Tse-ye-chee*	Cliff
Close	*Ul-chi-uh-nal-yah*	Close
Coast Guard	*Ta-bas-dsissi*	Shore Runner
Code	*Yil-tas*	Peck
Colon	*Naki-alh-deh-da-al-zhin*	Two Spots
Column	*Alth-kay-ne-zih*	Column
Combat	*Da-ah-hi-jih-ganh*	Fighting
Combination	*Al-tkas-ei*	Mixed
Come	*Huc-quo*	Come
Comma	*Tsa-na-dahl*	Tail Drop

WORD	NAVAJO	LITERAL TRANSLATION
Commercial	*Nai-el-ne-hi*	Commercial
Commit	*Huc-quo-la jish*	Come Glove
Communication	*Ha-neh-al-enji*	Making Talk
Conceal	*Be-ki-asz-jole*	Conceal
Concentration	*Ta-la-hi-jih*	One Place
Concussion	*Whe-hus-dil*	Concussion
Condition	*Ah-ho-tai*	How It Is
Conference	*Be-ke-ya-ti*	Talk Over
Confidential	*Na-nil-in*	Kept Secret
Confirm	*Ta-a-neh*	Make Sure
Conquer	*A-keh-des-dlin*	Won
Consider	*Ne-tsa-cas*	Think It Over
Consist	*Bilh (C)*	Consist
Consolidate	*Ah-hih-hi-nil*	Put Together
Construct	*Ahl-neh*	To Make
Contact	*Ah-hi-di-dail*	Come Together
Continue	*Ta-yi-teh*	Continue
Control	*Nai-ghiz*	Control
Convoy	*Tkal-kah-o-nel*	Moving On Water
Coordinate	*Beh-eh-ho-zin-na-as-dzoh*	Known Lines
Counter Attack	*Woltah-al-ki-gi-jeh*	Counter Act
Course	*Coh-joi-goh*	Course
Craft	*Ah-toh*	Nest
Creek	*Toh-nil-tsanh*	Very Little Water
Cross	*Al-n-as-dzoh*	Cross
Cub	*Shush-yahz*	Cub
Dash	*Us-dzoh*	Dash
Dawn	*Ha-yeli-kahn*	Dawn
Defense	*Ahh-kin-cil-toh*	Defense
Degree	*Nahl-kihd*	Degree
Delay	*Be-sitihn*	Deer Lay
Deliver	*Be-bih-zihde*	Deer Liver
Demotion	*Ah-deel-tahi*	Blow Up
Dense	*Ho-diilh-cla (D)*	Wet
Depart	*Da-de-yah*	Depart
Department	*Hogan*	Department
Designate	*Ye-khi-del-nei*	Point Out
Desperate	*Ah-da-ah-ho-dzah*	Down to Last
Detach	*Al-cha-nil*	Detached
Detail	*Be-beh-sha*	Detail

WORD	NAVAJO	LITERAL TRANSLATION
Detonator	*Ah-deel-tahi (Or)*	Blown Up
Difficult	*Na-ne-klah*	Difficult
Dig In	*Le-eh-gade*	Dig In
Direct	*Ah-ji-go*	Direct
Disembark	*Eh-ha-jay*	Get Out
Dispatch	*La-chai-en-seis-be-jay*	Dog Is Patch
Displace	*Hih-do-nal*	Move
Display	*Be-seis-na-neh*	Deer is Play
Disposition	*A-ho-tay*	Disposition
Distribute	*Nah-neh*	Distribute
District	*Be-thin-ya-ni-che*	Deer Ice Strict
Do	*Tse-le*	Small Pup
Document	*Beh-eh-ho-zinz (D)*	Document
Drive	*Ah-nol-kahl*	Drive
Dud	*Di-giss-yahzie*	Small Dummy
Dummy	*Di-giss-tso*	Big Dummy
Each	*Ta-lahi-ne-zini-go*	Each
Echelon	*Who-dzah*	Line
Edge	*Be-ba-hi*	Edge
Effective	*Be-delh-need*	Effective
Effort	*Yea-go*	With All Your Might
Element	*Ah-na-nai*	Troop Representing Others
Elevate	*Ali-khi-ho-ne-oha*	Elevate
Eliminate	*Ha-beh-to-dzil*	Eliminate
Embark	*Eh-ho-jay*	Get On
Emergency	*Ho-nez-cla*	Emergency
Emplacement	*La-az-nil*	Emplacement
Encircle	*Ye-nas-teh (E)*	Encircle
Encounter	*Bi-khanh*	Go Against
Engage	*A-ha-ne-ho-ta*	Agreed
Engine	*Chidi-bi-tsi-tsine (E)*	Engine
Engineer	*Day-dil-jah-he*	Engineer
Enlarge	*Nih-tsa-goh-al-neh*	Make Big
Enlist	*Bih-zih-a-da-yi-lah*	Enlist
Entire	*Ta-a-tah (E)*	Entire
Entrench	*E-gad-ah-ne-lih*	Make Ditch
Envelop	*A-zah-gi-ya*	Envelop
Equipment	*Ya-ha-de-tahi*	Equipment
Erect	*Yeh-zihn*	Stand Up
Escape	*Aj-zeh-ha-ge-yah*	Escape

Word	Navajo	Literal Translation
Establish	*Has-tay-dzah*	Establish
Estimate	*Bih-ke-tse-hod-des-kez*	Estimate
Evacuate	*Ha-na*	Evacuate
Except	*Neh-dih (E)*	Except
Expect	*Na-wol-ne*	Expect
Exchange	*Alh-nahl-yah*	Exchange
Execute	*A-do-nil*	Execute
Explosive	*Ah-del-tahi (E)*	Explosive
Expedite	*Shil-loh (E)*	Speed Up
Extend	*Ne-tdale*	Make Wide
Extreme	*Al-tsan-ah-bahm*	Each End
Fail	*Cha-al-eind*	Fail
Failure	*Yees-ghin*	Failure
Farm	*Mai-be-he-ahgan*	Fox Arm
Feed	*Dzeh-chi-yon*	Feed
Field	*Clo-dih (F)*	Field
Fierce	*Toh-bah-ha-zsid (F)*	Afraid
File	*Ba-eh-chez*	File
Final	*Tah-ah-kwo-dih*	That Is All
Flame Thrower	*Coh-ah-ghil-tlid*	Flame Thrower
Flank	*Dah-di-kad*	Flank
Flare	*Wo-chi*	Light Streak
Flight	*Ma-e-as-zloli*	Fox Light
Force	*Ta-na-ne-ladi*	Without Care
Form	*Be-cha*	Form
Formation	*Be-cha-ye-lailh*	Formation
Fortification	*Ah-na-sozi*	Cliff Dwelling
Fortify	*Ah-na-sozi-yazzie*	Small Fortification
Forward	*Tehi*	Let's Go
Fragmentation	*Besh-yazzie*	Small Metal
Frequency	*Ha-talhi-tso*	Big Singer
Friendly	*Neh-hecho-da-ne*	Friendly
From	*Bi-tsan-dehn*	From
Furnish	*Yeas-nil (F)*	Furnish
Further	*Wo-nas-di*	Further
Garrison	*Yah-a-da-hal-yon-ih*	Take Care Of
Gasoline	*Chidi-bi-toh*	Gasoline
Grenade	*Ni-ma-si*	Potatoes
Guard	*Ni-dih-da-hi*	Guard
Guide	*Nah-e-thlai*	Guide

WORD	NAVAJO	LITERAL TRANSLATION
Hall	*Lhi-ta-a-ta*	Horse All
Half Track	*Alh-nih-jah-a-quhe*	Race Track
Halt	*Ta-akwai-i*	Halt
Handle	*Bet-seen*	Handle
Have	*Jo*	Have
Headquarter	*Na-ha-tah-ba-hogan*	Headquarter
Held	*Wo-tah*	Held (Past Tense)
High	*Wo-tah*	High
High Explosive	*Be-al-doh-be-ca-bih-dzil-igi*	Powerful Shell
Highway	*Wo-tah-ho-ne-teh*	High Way
Hold	*Wo-tkanh*	Hold
Hospital	*A-zey-al-ih*	Place of Medicine
Hostile	*A-nah-ne-dzin*	Not Friendly
Howitzer	*Be-el-don-tso-quodi*	Short Big Gun
Illuminate	*Wo-chi (I)*	Light Up
Immediately	*Shil-loh (I)*	Immediately
Impact	*A-he-dis-goh*	Impact
Important	*Ba-has-teh*	Important
Improve	*Ho-dol-zhond*	Improve
Include	*El-tsod*	Include
Increase	*Ho-nalh*	Increase
Indicate	*Ba-hal-neh*	Tell About
Infantry	*Ta-neh-nal-dahi*	Infantry
Infiltrate	*Ye-gha-ne-jeh*	Went Through
Initial	*Beh-ed-de-dlid*	Brand
Install	*Ehd-tnah*	Install
Installation	*Nas-nil*	In Place
Instruct	*Na-ne-tgin*	Teach
Intelligence	*Ho-yah (I)*	Smart
Intense	*Dzeel*	Strength
Intercept	*Yel-na-me-jah*	Intercept
Interfere	*Ah-nilh-khlai*	Interfere
Interpret	*Ah-tah-ha-ne*	Interpret
Investigate	*Na-ali-ka*	Track
Involve	*A-tah*	Involve
Is	*Seis*	Seven
Island	*Seis-keyah*	Seven Island
Isolate	*Bih-tsa-nel-kad*	Separate
Jungle	*Woh-di-chil*	Jungle

WORD	NAVAJO	LITERAL TRANSLATION
Kill	*Naz-tsaid*	Kill
Kilocycle	*Nas-tsaid-a-kha-ah-yeh-ha-dilh*	Kill Oil Go Around
Labor	*Na-nish*	Labor
Word	*Navajo*	Literal Translation
Land	*Kay-yah*	Land
Launch	*Tka-ghil-zhod*	Launch
Leader	*Ah-na-ghai*	Leader
Least	*De-be-yazie-ha-a-ah*	Lamb East
Leave	*Dah-de-yah*	He Left
Left	*Nish-cla-jih-goh*	Left
Less	*Bi-oh (L)*	Less
Level	*Dil-konh*	Level
Liaison	*Da-a-he-gi-eneh*	Know Other's Action
Limit	*Ba-has-ah*	Limit
Litter	*Ni-das-ton (L)*	Scatter
Locate	*A-kwe-eh*	Spot
Loss	*Ut-din*	Loss
Machine Gun	*A-knah-as-donih*	Rapid Fire Gun
Magnetic	*Na-e-lahi*	Pick Up
Manage	*Hastni-beh-na-hai*	Man Age
Maneuver	*Na-na-o-nalth*	Moving Around
Map	*Kah-ya-nesh-chai*	Map
Maximum	*Bel-dil-khon*	Fill To Top
Mechanic	*Chiti-a-nayl-inih*	Auto Repairman
Mechanized	*Chidi-da-ah-he-goni*	Fighting Cars
Medical	*A-zay*	Medicine
Megacycle	*Mil-ah-heh-ah-dilh*	Million Go Around
Merchant Ship	*Na-el-nehi-tsin-na-ailh*	Merchant Ship
Message	*Hane-al-neh*	Message
Military	*Silago-keh-goh*	Military
Millimeter	*Na-as-tso-si-a-ye-do-tish*	Double Mouse
Mine	*Ha-gade*	Mine
Minimum	*Be-oh (M)*	Minimum
Minute	*Ah-khay-el-kit-yazzie*	Little Hour
Mission	*Ai-neshodi*	Mission
Mistake	*O-zhi*	Miss
Mopping	*Ha-tao-di*	Mopping
More	*Thla-na-nah*	More

Word	Navajo	Literal Translation
Mortar	*Be-al-doh-cid-da-hi*	Sitting Gun
Motion	*Na-hot-nah*	Motion
Motor	*Chide-be-tse-tsen*	Car Head
Native	*Ka-ha-teni*	Native
Navy	*Tal-kah-silago*	Sea Soldier
Necessary	*Ye-na-zehn*	Want
Negative	*Do-ya-sho-da*	No Good
Net	*Na-nes-dizi*	Net
Neutral	*Do-neh-lini*	Neutral
Normal	*Doh-a-ta-h-dah*	Normal
Not	*Ni-dah-than-zie*	No Turkey
Notice	*Ne-da-tazi-thin*	No Turkey Ice
Now	*Kut (N)*	Now
Number	*Beh-bih-ke-as-chinigih*	What's Written
Objective	*Bi-ne-yei*	Goal
Observe	*Hal-zid*	Observe
Obstacle	*Da-ho-desh-zha*	Obstacle
Occupy	*Yeel-tsod*	Taken
Of	*Toh-ni-tkal-lo*	Ocean Fish
Offensive	*Bin-kie-jinh-jih-dez-jay*	Offensive
Once	*Ta-lai-di*	Once
Only	*Ta-ei-tay-a-yah*	Only
Operate	*Ye-nahl-nish*	Work At
Opportunity	*Ash-ga-alin*	Opportunity
Opposition	*Ne-he-tsah-jih-shin*	Opposition
Or	*Eh-dodah-goh*	Either
Orange	*Tchil-lhe-soi*	Orange
Order	*Be-eh-ho-zini*	Order
Ordnance	*Lei-az-jah*	Under Ground
Originate	*Das-teh-do (O)*	Begin
Other	*La-e-cih*	Other
Out	*Clo-dih (O)*	Out Side
Overlay	*Be-ka-has-tsoz*	Overlay
Parenthesis	*Atsanh*	Rib
Particular	*A-yo-ad-do-neh*	Particular
Party	*Da-sha-jah (P)*	Party
Pay	*Na-eli-ya*	Pay
Penalize	*Tah-ni-des-tanh*	Set Bank
Percent	*Yal*	Money (All Sorts)

WORD	NAVAJO	LITERAL TRANSLATION
Period	*Da-ahl-zhin*	Period
Periodic	*Da-al-zhin-thin-moasi*	Periodic
Permit	*Gos-shi-e (P)*	Permit
Personnel	*Da-ne-lei*	Member
Photograph	*Beh-chi-ma-had-nil*	Photograph
Pill Box	*Bi-so-dih-dot-sahi-bi-tsah*	Sick Pig Box
Pinned Down	*Bil-dah-has-tanh-ya*	Pinned Down
Plane	*Tsidi*	Bird
Plasma	*Dil-di-ghili*	Plasma
Point	*Be-so-de-dez-ahe*	Pig Point
Pontoon	*Tkosh-jah-da-na-elt*	Floating Barrel
Position	*Bilh-has-ahn*	Position
Possible	*Ta-ha-ah-tay*	Possible
Post	*Sah-dei*	Post
Prepare	*Hash-tay-ho-dit-ne*	Prepare
Present	*Kut (P)*	Present
Previous	*Bih-tse-dih (P)*	Previous
Primary	*Altseh-nan-day-hi-gih*	1st Position
Priority	*Hane-pesodi*	Priority
Probable	*Da-tsi*	Probable
Problem	*Na-nish-tsoh*	Big Job
Proceed	*Nay-nih-jih*	Go
Progress	*Nah-sai (P)*	Progress
Protect	*Ah-chanh*	Self Defense
Provide	*Yis-nil (P)*	Provide
Purple	*Dinl-chi*	Purple
Pyrotechnic	*Coh-na-chanh*	Fancy Fire
Question	*Ah-jah*	Ear
Quick	*Shil-loh*	Quick
Radar	*Esat-tsanh (R)*	Listen
Raid	*Dezjay*	Raid
Railhead	*A-de-geh-hi*	Shipping Point
Railroad	*Konh-na-al-bansi-bi-thin*	Railroad
Rallying	*A-lah-na-o-glalth*	Gathering
Range	*An-zah*	Distance
Rate	*Gah-eh-yahn*	Rabbit Ate
Ration	*Na-a-jah*	Ration
Ravine	*Chush-ka (R)*	Ravine
Reach	*Il-day (R)*	Reach
Ready	*Kut (R)*	Ready

WORD	NAVAJO	LITERAL TRANSLATION
Rear	*Be-ka-denh (R)*	Rear
Receipt	*Shoz-teh*	Receipt
Recommend	*Che-ho-tai-tahn*	Recommend
Reconnaissance	*Ha-a-cidi*	Inspector
Reconnoiter	*Ta-ah-ne-al-ya*	Make Sure
Record	*Cah-ah-nah-kloli*	Re-rope
Red	*Li-chi*	Red
Reef	*Tsa-zhin*	Black Rock
Re-embark	*Eh-na-jay*	Go In
Refire	*Na-na-coh*	Refire
Regulate	*Na-yel-na*	Regulate
Reinforce	*Nal-dzil*	Reinforce
Relief	*Aganh-tol-jay*	Relief
Relieve	*Nah-jih-co-nal-ya*	Remove
Reorganize	*Ha-dit-zah*	Reorganize
Replacement	*Ni-na-do-nil*	Replacement
Report	*Who-neh*	Got Word
Representative	*Tka-naz-nili*	Triple Men
Request	*Jo-kayed-goh*	Ask For
Reserve	*Hesh-j-e*	Reserve
Restrict	*Ba-ho-chinh*	Restrict
Retire	*Ah-hos-teend*	Retire
Retreat	*Ji-din-nes-chanh*	Retreat
Return	*Na-dzah*	Came Back
Reveal	*Who-neh (L)*	Reveal
Revert	*Na-si-yiz*	Turn About
Revetment	*Ba-nas-cla (R)*	Corner
Ridge	*Gah-ghil-keid*	Rabbit Ridge
Riflemen	*Be-al-do-hosteen*	Riflemen
River	*Toh-yil-kal*	Much Water
Robot Bomb	*A-ye-shi-na-tah-ih*	Egg Fly
Rocket	*Lesz-yil-beshi*	Sand Boil
Roll	*Yeh-mas*	Roll
Round	*Naz-pas (R)*	Round
Route	*Gah-bih-tkeen*	Rabbit Trail
Runner	*Nih-dzid-teih*	Runner
Sabotage	*A-tkel-yah*	Hindered
Saboteur	*A-tkel-el-ini*	Trouble Maker
Sailor	*Cha-le-gai*	White Caps
Salvage	*Na-has-glah*	Pick Them Up
Sat	*Bih-la-sana-cid-da-hi*	Apple Sitting

| --- | --- | --- |
Scarlet & Red	*Lhe-chi (S &R)*	Red
Schedule	*Beh-eh-ho-zini*	Schedule
Scout	*Ha-a-sid-al-sizi-gih*	Short Recon.
Screen	*Besh-na-nes-dizi*	Screen
Seaman	*Tkal-kah-dineh-ih*	Seaman
Secret	*Bah-has-tkih*	Secret
Sector	*Yoehi (S)*	Sector
Secure	*Ye-dzhe-al-tsis-gi*	Small Security
Seize	*Yeel-stod (s)*	Seize
Select	*Be-tah-has-gla*	Took Out
Semicolon	*Da-ahl-zhin-bi-tsa-na-dahl*	Dot Drop
Set	*Dzeh-cid-da-hi*	Elk Sitting
Shackle	*Di-bah-nesh-gohz (S)*	Shackle
Shell	*Be-al-doh-be-ca*	Shell
Shore	*Tah-bahn (S)*	Shore
Short	*Bosh-keesh*	Short
Side	*Bosh-keesh*	Side
Sight	*Ye-el-tsanh*	Seen
Signal	*Na-eh-eh-gish*	By Signs
Simplex	*Alah-ih-ne-tih*	Inner Wire
Sit	*Tkin-cid-da-hi*	Ice Sitting
Situate	*A-ho-tay (S)*	Situate
Smoke	*Lit*	Smoke
Sniper	*Oh-behi*	Pick 'em Off
Space	*Be-tkah*	Between
Special	*E-yih-sih*	Main Thing
Speed	*Yo-zons*	Swift Motion
Sporadic	*Ah-na-ho-neil*	Now and Then
Spotter	*Eel-tsay-i*	Spotter
Spray	*Klesh-so-dilzin*	Snake Pray
Squadron	*Nah-ghizi*	Squash
Storm	*Ne-ol*	Storm
Strafe	*Na-wo-ghi-goid*	Hoe
Straggler	*Chy-ne-de-dahe*	Straggler
Strategy	*Na-ha-tah (S)*	Strategy
Stream	*Toh-ni-lih*	Running Water
Strength	*Dzhel*	Strength
Stretch	*Desz-tsood*	Stretch
Strike	*Nay-dal-ghal*	Strike
Strip	*Ha-tih-jah*	Strip
Stubborn	*Nil-ta*	Stubborn

Word	Navajo	Literal Translation
Subject	*Na-nish-yazzie*	Small Job
Submerge	*Tkal-cla-yi-yah*	Went Under Water
Submit	*A-nih-leh*	Send
Subordinate	*Al-khi-nal-dzl*	Helping Each Other
Succeed	*Yah-taygo-e-elah*	Make Good
Success	*Ut-zah*	It Is Done
Successful	*Ut-zah-ha-dez-bin*	It Is Done Well
Successive	*Ut-zah-sid*	Success Scar
Such	*Yis-cleh*	Sox
Suffer	*To-ho-ne*	Suffer
Summary	*Shinh-go-bah*	Summer Mary
Supplementary	*Tka-go-ne-nan-dey-he*	3rd Position
Supply	*Nal-yeh-hi*	Supply
Supply Ship	*Nalga-hi-tsin-nah-ailh*	Supply Ship
Support	*Ba-ah-hot-gli*	Depend
Surrender	*Ne-na-cha*	Surrender
Surround	*Naz-pas (S)*	Surround
Survive	*Yis-da-ya*	Survive
System	*Di-ba-tsa-as-zhi-bi-tsin*	System
Tactical	*E-chihn*	Tactical
Take	*Gah-tahn*	Take
Tank	*Chay-da-gahi*	Tortoise
Tank Destroyer	*Chay-da-gahi-nail-tsaidi*	Tortoise Killer
Target	*Wol-doni*	Target
Task	*Tazi-na-eh-dil-kid*	Turkey Ask
Team	*Deh-na-as-tso-si*	Tea Mouse
Terrace	*Ali-khi-ho-ne-oha (T)*	Terrace
Terrain	*Tashi-na-hal-thin*	Turkey Rain
Territory	*Ka-yah (T)*	Territory
That	*Tazi-cha*	Turkey Hat
The	*Cha-gee*	Blue-jay
Their	*Bih*	Their
Thereafter	*Ta-zi-kwa-i-be-ka-di*	Turkey Here After
These	*Cha-gi-o-eh*	The See
They	*Cha-gee (Y)*	They
This	*Di*	This
Together	*Ta-bilh*	Together
Torpedo	*Lo-be-ca*	Fish Shell
Total	*Ta-al-so (T)*	Total
Tracer	*Beh-na-al-kah-hi*	Tracer
Traffic Diagram	*Hane-ba-na-as-dzoh*	Diagram Story Line

WORD	NAVAJO	LITERAL TRANSLATION
Train	*Coh-nai-ali-bahn-si*	Train
Transportation	*A-hah-da-a-cha*	Transportation
Trench	*E-gade*	Trench
Triple	*Tka-ih*	Triple
Troop	*Nal-deh-hi*	Troop
Truck	*Chido-tso*	Big Auto
Type	*Alth-ah-a-teh (T)*	Type
Under	*Bi-yah*	Under
Unidentified	*Do-bay-hosen-e*	Unidentified
Unit	*Da-az-jah (U)*	Unit
Unshackle	*No-da-eh-nesh-gohz*	U-shackle
Until	*Uh-quo-ho*	Until
Vicinity	*Na-hos-ah-gih*	There About
Village	*Chah-ho-oh-lhan-ih*	Many Shelter
Visibility	*Nay-es-tee*	Visibility
Vital	*Ta-eh-ye-sy*	Vital
Warning	*Bilh-he-neh (W)*	Warning
Was	*Ne-teh*	Was
Water	*Tkoh*	Water
Wave	*Yilh-kolh*	Wave
Weapon	*Beh-dah-a-hi-jih-gani*	Fighting Weapon
Well	*To-ha-ha-dlay*	Well
When	*Gloe-eh-na-ah-wo-hai*	Weasel Hen
Where	*Gloe-ih-qui-ah*	Weasel Here
Which	*Gloe-ih-a-hsi-tlon*	Weasel Tied Together
Will	*Gloe-ih-dot-sahi*	Sick Weasel
Wire	*Besh-tsosie*	Small Wire
With	*Bilh (W)*	With
Within	*Bilh-bigih*	With In
Without	*Ta-gaid*	Without
Wood	*Chiz*	Fire Wood
Wound	*Cah-da-khi*	Wound
Yard	*A-del-tahl*	Yard
Zone	*Bih-na-has-dzoh*	Zone

Appendix D

Map Showing Navajo Nation Land

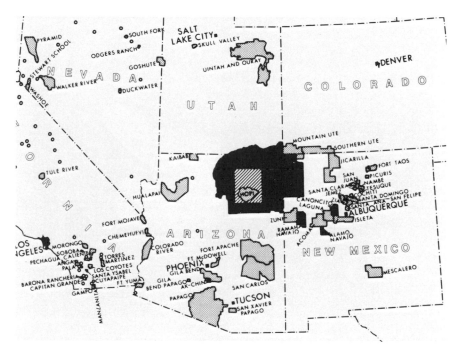

On the map above, the black area shows the present Navajo Nation land; the diagonal shaded area is the disputed area between Navajo and Hopi tribes; the area labeled "Hopi" is the landlocked Hopi Reservation within the Navajo Nation land; other areas not applicable to the subject in the book are also marked.

The author is indebted to the University of Oklahoma for granting permission to reprint the above map from The Navajo Atlas © by James Goodman, published by the University of Oklahoma Press, Norman, Oklahoma, 1982

Index

C

C-rations, *see food*
California 6
Camp Elliott 40, 41, 42, 61, 64
Camp Pendleton 57, 66, 71, 76
Canada xi, 9, 44
canals, irrigation 8
Canyon de Chelly 5, 6, 14, 55, 92
Cape Glouster 78,79
Carleton, General James H. 14, 55
Carson, Kit 14, 55
Cattlechaser, Dennis 79
ceremony (ies) 16
    blessing the hogan 31
    Enemy Way 95
    Gourd Dance 96
    healing 31, 32, 94
        sandpainting 27, 31, 32, 33,
            35, 94
    marriage 31
    Squaw Dance 94, 95, 96
    war 96
    womanhood 31
    Yé'ii Bicheii 11, 75
Chaco Canyon 4, 92
Chavez, George 80
child, Navajo-speaking xviii
children xviii, 7, 14, 17, 18, 21, 22,
        23, 25, 37, 44, 47, 112, 117
children, Navajo xii
children, raising 118
China xi, 88
    Mongolian 9
    Tientsin 79
Chinese xi
Chippewa 132
Choctaws 38
Christian 14
cipher 40
    devices 38
    makers 37
Circle of Life 11
civilization, ancient 4
clan (s) 7, 27, 62
    father's 27

clan (continued)
    mother's 27
    names 28
    relationships 27
    system 27
    Towering House 7
Claw, Grayson 115
Claw, Thomas 115
Cleveland, Bennie 78
climate 3, 6
clothes 10
coal 24
Code, *see Navajo Code*
code xii, 37, 38, 40, 42, 44, 45, 51,
      119
    Indian words 40
    language-usage 39
    message sticks 37
    method 49, 76
    name 49
    Navajo 39
    Navajo names 43
    numbers 71
    never broken 39
    original 71
    other language 34
    semaphore flags 52
    smoke signals 37
    within a code 44
code talkers iii
code words 49, 75
Code Talkers Association, *see*
    Navajo Code Talkers
    Association
College, Navajo Community Col-
    lege (*see Diné College*)
Colorado 3, 111
Colter, Brenda xvii
Columbus Day xiii
Comanches 37, 38
coming out 36
communication 13, 38, 47, 50
    devices, blinkers 47, 52
    front line 50
    Morse Code 47, 52

communication (continued)
    numbers 61
    radio 38, 40, 52, 57, 64, 65, 78,
        79, 83, 85, 86, 105
    secret 39
    semaphore 47, 52
    telephone 40, 52
    unable to sabotage 83
    verbal 37
    walkie-talkie (s)64,52
Conner, Maj. Howard M. 70, 86
contracts, government 114
copper bells 6
Coral Sea, battle of 77, 89
corn, growing 4
Coronado, Francisco Vasquez de 9
corridor, ice-free 8
Council, Tribal 100
Crawford, Dan xix
crime, killings 114
crop failure 4
Crow Canyon Archaeological Cen-
        ter xx, 117
cryptographers 64
cryptography 38, 88
cults, satanic 114
cultural
    adjustments xix
    differences xviii, 119
    experience 95
    understanding 117
culture xi, xiv, xvii, xix, 3, 6, 16, 18,
        45, 61, 62, 75, 91, 100, 103,
        116, 117
    conflict of 113
    shock 115
    Anglo war xii
    Indian 92
    mythical 26
    Navajo 58, 102

D
Daltons, Karl and Etta xviii
Dances With Wolves (movie)118
dancing 31
Dawkins, James xix

death, Navajo attitude towards 26
decipher 37, 44, 49
Dedication iii
deities 16
Denetdale, Myron and Virginia 103
diagnosis of illness 31
diagnostician (s) 31
    Star Gazer xviii, 31
    Trembling Hand xviii, 31
dictionary, "The Navajo Code" 143
Diné xi, xvii, 3, 9, 12, 110, 111
Diné College xix, 14, 91, 97, 99,
        112
disease 4, 31, 114
    arthritis 4
    tuberculosis 114
Dobrinen, Dabah xix
doctor xviii, 97
    first female Navajo 114
    Navajo medical 21, 31, 97
dogs 4
    use of war 125
Doris Duke Oral History Project
        xxi, 39, 67, 89
drought xi, 6

E
East, door always faces 22
    god of the 22
education 17, 42, 63, 112, 117
    boarding school 61, 112, 115
    college 112
    four-year college degree 113
    free English 17
    GI Bill 97, 98
    graduate school 113
    grammar school 133
    grants 100
    guidance counselors 118
    language 45
    opportunities 97, 98
    public schools 112
    school 114
    schools of higher grades 133
    teachers 112, 116, 118
    vowels 45

THIS BOOK PRINTED BY

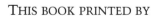

OF PORTLAND, MAINE

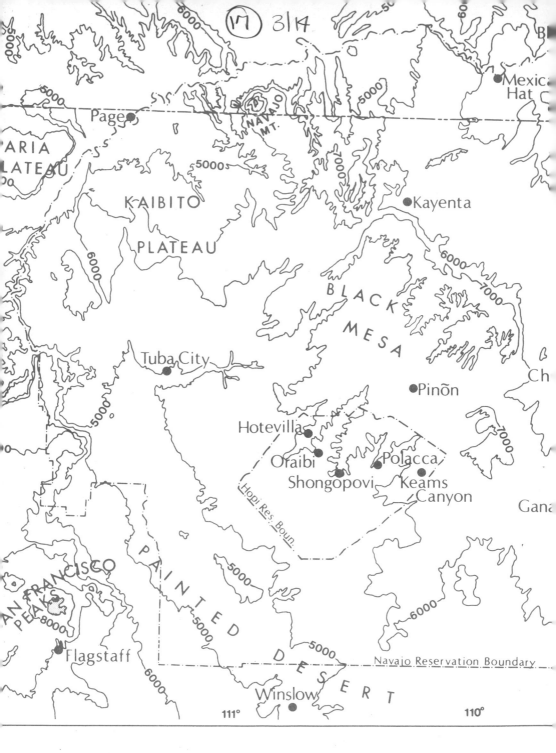

Mexic
Hat

B

Page

PARIA
PLATEAU
Oo

5000

5000

NAVAJO
MT.

KAIBITO

PLATEAU

Kayenta

5000

6000

7000

B L A C K

M E S A

6000

7000

Ch

6000

Tuba City

Pinõn

7000

Hotevilla

Oraibi

Polacca

Shongopovi

Keams
Canyon

Hopi Res. Boun.

Gan

AN FRANCISCO
PEAKS
8000

P A I N T E D

5000

5000

6000

5000

5000

6000

Flagstaff

6000

D E S E R T

Navajo Reservation Boundary

Winslow

111°

110°

Areas above 10,000 feet (3000 meters)

Note: 4000 and 9000 foot (1200 and 2750 meter) contours not shown

Map 14

Stream